# OLD-FASHIONED FA

## BY

Juliana Horatia Gatty Ewing

# OLD-FASHIONED FAIRY TALES

**Published by Mythik Press**

**New York City, NY**

**First published circa 1885**

**Copyright © Mythik Press, 2015**

# ABOUT MYTHIK PRESS

From the moment people first began practicing rituals, they have been creating folk tales and legends to celebrate their past and create a unique cultural identity. Mythik Press carries these legacies forward by publishing the greatest stories ever concocted, from King Arthur to the fairy tales of the Brothers Grimm.

**JULIANA HORATIA EWING.**

LONDON:
SOCIETY FOR PROMOTING CHRISTIAN KNOWLEDGE,
NORTHUMBERLAND AVENUE, W.C.
NEW YORK: E. & J.B. YOUNG & CO.
[Published under the direction of the General Literature Committee.]

UNDINE MARCIA GATTY.   DEDICATED

J.H.E.

"Know'st thou not the little path That winds about the Ferny brae, That is the road to bonnie Elfland, Where thou and I this night maun gae."

Thomas the Rhymer.

## PREFACE.

As the title of this story-book may possibly suggest that the tales are old fairy tales told afresh, it seems well to explain that this is not so.

Except for the use of common "properties" of Fairy Drama, and a scrupulous endeavour to conform to tradition in local colour and detail, the stories are all new.

They have appeared at intervals during some years past in "Aunt Judy's Magazine for Young People," and were written in conformity to certain theories respecting stories of this kind, with only two of which shall the kindly reader of prefaces be troubled.

First, that there are ideas and types, occurring in the myths of all countries, which are common properties, to use which does not lay the teller of fairy tales open to the charge of plagiarism. Such as the idea of the weak outwitting the strong; the failure of man to choose wisely when he may have his wish; or the desire of sprites to exchange their careless and unfettered existence for the pains and penalties of humanity, if they may thereby share in the hopes of the human soul.

Secondly, that in these household stories (the models for which were originally oral tradition) the thing most to be avoided is a discursive or descriptive style of writing. Brevity and epigram must ever be soul of their wit, and they should be written as tales that are told.

The degree in which, if at all, the following tales fulfil these conditions, nursery critics must decide.

There are older critics before whom fairy tales, as such, need excuse, even if they do not meet with positive disapprobation.

On this score I can only say that, for myself, I believe them to be—beyond all need of defence—most valuable literature for the young. I do not believe that wonder-tales confuse children's ideas of truth. If there are young intellects so imperfect as to be incapable of distinguishing between fancy and falsehood, it is surely most desirable to develop in them the power to do so; but, as a rule, in childhood we appreciate the distinction with a vivacity which, as elders, our care-clogged memories fail to recall.

Moreover fairy tales have positive uses in education, which no cramming of facts, and no merely domestic fiction can serve.

Like Proverbs and Parables, they deal with first principles under the simplest forms. They convey knowledge of the world, shrewd lessons of virtue and vice, of common sense and sense of humour, of the seemly and the absurd, of pleasure and pain, success and failure, in narratives where the plot moves briskly and dramatically from a beginning to an end. They treat, not of the corner of a nursery or a playground, but of the world at large, and life in perspective; of forces visible and invisible; of Life, Death, and Immortality.

For causes obvious to the student of early myths, they foster sympathy with nature, and no class of child-literature has done so much to inculcate the love of animals.

They cultivate the Imagination, that great gift which time and experience lead one more and more to value—handmaid of Faith, of Hope, and, perhaps most of all, of Charity!

It is true that some of the old fairy tales do not teach the high and useful lessons that most of them do; and that they unquestionably deal now and again with phases of grown-up life, and with crimes and catastrophes, that seem unsuitable for nursery entertainment.

As to the latter question, it must be remembered that the brevity of the narrative—whether it be a love story or a robber story—deprives it of all harm; a point which writers of modern fairy tales do not always realize for their guidance.

The writer of the following tales has endeavoured to bear this principle in mind, and it is hoped that the morals—and it is of the essence of fairy tales to have a moral—of all of them are beyond reproach.

For the rest they are committed to the indulgence of the gentle reader.

Hans Anderssen, perhaps the greatest writer of modern fairy tales, was content to say:

"Fairy Tale Never Dies."

J. H. E.

## GOOD LUCK IS BETTER THAN GOLD.

There was once upon a time a child who had Good Luck for his godfather.

"I am not Fortune," said Good Luck to the parents; "I have no gifts to bestow, but whenever he needs help I will be at hand."

"Nothing could be better," said the old couple. They were delighted. But what pleases the father often fails to satisfy the son: moreover, every man thinks that he deserves just a little more than he has got, and does not reckon it to the purpose if his father had less.

Many a one would be thankful to have as good reasons for contentment as he who had Good Luck for his godfather.

If he fell, Good Luck popped something soft in the way to break his fall; if he fought, Good Luck directed his blows, or tripped up his adversary; if he got into a scrape, Good Luck helped him out of it; and if ever Misfortune met him, Good Luck contrived to hustle her on the pathway till his godson got safely by.

In games of hazard the godfather played over his shoulder. In matters of choice he chose for him. And when the lad began to work on his father's farm the farmer began to get rich. For no bird or field-mouse touched a seed that his son had sown, and every plant he planted throve when Good Luck smiled on it.

The boy was not fond of work, but when he did go into the fields, Good Luck followed him.

"Your christening-day was a blessed day for us all," said the old farmer.

"He has never given me so much as a lucky sixpence," muttered Good Luck's godson.

"I am not Fortune—I make no presents," said the godfather.

When we are discontented it is oftener to please our neighbours than ourselves. It was because the other boys had said—"Simon, the shoemaker's son, has an alderman for his godfather. He gave him a silver spoon with the Apostle Peter for the handle; but thy godfather is more powerful than any alderman"—that Good Luck's godson complained, "He has never given me so much as a bent sixpence."

By and by the old farmer died, and his son grew up, and had the largest farm in the country. The other boys grew up also, and as they looked over the farmer's boundary-wall, they would say:

"Good-morning, Neighbour. That is certainly a fine farm of yours. Your cattle thrive without loss. Your crops grow in the rain and are reaped with the sunshine. Mischance never comes your road. What you have worked for you enjoy. Such success would turn the heads of poor folk like us. At the same time one would think a man need hardly work for his living at all who has Good Luck for his godfather."

"That is very true," thought the farmer. "Many a man is prosperous, and reaps what he sows, who had no more than the clerk and the sexton for gossips at his christening."

"What is the matter, Godson?" asked Good Luck, who was with him in the field.

"I want to be rich," said the farmer.

"You will not have to wait long," replied the godfather. "In every field you sow, in every flock you rear there is increase without abatement. Your wealth is already tenfold greater than your father's."

"Aye, aye," replied the farmer. "Good wages for good work. But many a young man has gold at his command who need never turn a sod, and none of the Good People came to his christening. Fortunatus's Purse now, or even a sack or two of gold—"

"Peace!" cried the godfather; "I have said that I give no gifts."

Though he had not Fortunatus's Purse, the farmer had now money and to spare, and when the harvest was gathered in, he bought a fine suit of clothes, and took his best horse and went to the royal city to see the sights.

The pomp and splendour, the festivities and fine clothes dazzled him.

"This is a gay life which these young courtiers lead," said he. "A man has nothing to do but to enjoy himself."

"If he has plenty of gold in his pocket," said a bystander.

By and by the Princess passed in her carriage. She was the King's only daughter. She had hair made of sunshine, and her eyes were stars.

"What an exquisite creature!" cried the farmer. "What would not one give to possess her?"

"She has as many suitors as hairs on her head," replied the bystander. "She wants to marry the Prince of Moonshine, but he only dresses in silver, and the King thinks he might find a richer son-in-law. The Princess will go to the highest bidder."

"And I have Good Luck for my godfather, and am not even at court!" cried the farmer; and he put spurs to his horse, and rode home.

Good Luck was taking care of the farm.

"Listen, Godfather!" cried the young man. "I am in love with the King's daughter, and want her to wife."

"It is not an easy matter," replied Good Luck, "but I will do what I can for you. Say that by good luck you saved the Princess's life, or perhaps better the King's—for they say he is selfish—"

"Tush!" cried the farmer. "The King is covetous, and wants a rich son-in-law."

"A wise man may bring wealth to a kingdom with his head, if not with his hands," said Good Luck, "and I can show you a district where the earth only wants mining to be flooded with wealth. Besides, there are a thousand opportunities that can be turned to account and influence. By wits and work, and with Good Luck to help him, many a poorer man than you has risen to greatness."

"Wits and work!" cried the indignant godson. "You speak well—truly! A hillman would have made a better godfather. Give me as much gold as will fill three meal-bins, and you may keep the rest of your help for those who want it."

Now at this moment by Good Luck stood Dame Fortune. She likes handsome young men, and there was some little jealousy between her and the godfather so she smiled at the quarrel.

"You would rather have had me for your gossip?" said she.

"If you would give me three wishes, I would," replied the farmer boldly, "and I would trouble you no more."

"Will you make him over to me?" said Dame Fortune to the godfather.

"If he wishes it," replied Good Luck. "But if he accepts your gifts he has no further claim on me."

"Nor on me either," said the Dame. "Hark ye, young man, you mortals are apt to make a hobble of your three wishes, and you may end with a sausage at your nose, like your betters."

"I have thought of it too often," replied the farmer, "and I know what I want. For my first wish I desire imperishable beauty."

"It is yours," said Dame Fortune, smiling as she looked at him.

"The face of a prince and the manners of a clown are poor partners," said the farmer. "My second wish is for suitable learning and courtly manners, which cannot be gained at the plough-tail."

"You have them in perfection," said the Dame, as the young man thanked her by a graceful bow.

"Thirdly," said he, "I demand a store of gold that I can never exhaust."

"I will lead you to it," said Dame Fortune; and the young man was so eager to follow her that he did not even look back to bid farewell to his godfather.

He was soon at court. He lived in the utmost pomp. He had a suit of armour made for himself out of beaten gold. No metal less precious might come near his person, except for the blade of his sword. This was obliged to be made of steel, for gold is not always strong enough to defend one's life or his honour. But the Princess still loved the Prince of Moonshine.

"Stuff and nonsense!" said the King. "I shall give you to the Prince of Gold."

"I wish I had the good luck to please her," muttered the young Prince. But he had not, for all his beauty and his wealth. However, she was to marry him, and that was something.

The preparations for the wedding were magnificent.

"It is a great expense," sighed the King, "but then I get the Prince of Gold for a son-in-law."

The Prince and his bride drove round the city in a triumphal procession. Her hair fell over her like sunshine, but the starlight of her eyes was cold.

In the train rode the Prince of Moonshine, dressed in silver, and with no colour in his face.

As the bridal chariot approached one of the city gates, two black ravens hovered over it, and then flew away, and settled on a tree.

Good Luck was sitting under the tree to see his godson's triumph, and he heard the birds talking above him.

"Has the Prince of Gold no friend who can tell him that there is a loose stone above the archway that is tottering to fall?" said they. And Good Luck covered his face with his mantle as the Prince drove through.

Just as they were passing out of the gateway the stone fell on to the Prince's head. He wore a casque of pure gold, but his neck was broken.

"We can't have all this expense for nothing," said the King: so he married his daughter to the Prince of Moonshine. If one can't get gold one must be content with silver.

"Will you come to the funeral?" asked Dame Fortune of the godfather.

"Not I," replied Good Luck. "I had no hand in this matter."

The rain came down in torrents. The black feathers on the ravens' backs looked as if they had been oiled.

"Caw! caw!" said they. "It was an unlucky end."

However, the funeral was a very magnificent one, for there was no stint of gold.

# THE HILLMAN AND THE HOUSEWIFE.

It is well known that the Good People cannot abide meanness. They like to be liberally dealt with when they beg or borrow of the human race; and, on the other hand, to those who come to them in need, they are invariably generous.

Now there once lived a certain Housewife who had a sharp eye to her own interests in temporal matters, and gave alms of what she had no use for, for the good of her soul. One day a Hillman knocked at her door.

"Can you lend us a saucepan, good Mother?" said he. "There's a wedding in the hill, and all the pots are in use."

"Is he to have one?" asked the servant lass who had opened the door.

"Aye, to be sure," answered the Housewife. "One must be neighbourly."

But when the maid was taking a saucepan from the shelf, she pinched her arm, and whispered sharply—"Not that, you slut! Get the old one out of the cupboard. It leaks, and the Hillmen are so neat, and such nimble workers, that they are sure to mend it before they send it home. So one obliges the Good People, and saves sixpence in tinkering. But you'll never learn to be notable whilst your head is on your shoulders."

Thus reproached, the maid fetched the saucepan, which had been laid by till the tinker's next visit, and gave it to the dwarf, who thanked her, and went away.

In due time the saucepan was returned, and, as the Housewife had foreseen, it was neatly mended and ready for use.

At supper-time the maid filled the pan with milk, and set it on the fire for the children's supper. But in a few minutes the milk was so burnt and smoked that no one could touch it, and even the pigs refused the wash into which it was thrown.

"Ah, good-for-nothing hussy!" cried the Housewife, as she refilled the pan herself, "you would ruin the richest with your carelessness. There's a whole quart of good milk wasted at once!"

"And that's twopence," cried a voice which seemed to come from the chimney, in a whining tone, like some nattering, discontented old body going over her grievances.

The Housewife had not left the saucepan for two minutes, when the milk boiled over, and it was all burnt and smoked as before.

"The pan must be dirty," muttered the good woman, in great vexation; "and there are two full quarts of milk as good as thrown to the dogs."

"And that's fourpence," added the voice in the chimney.

After a thorough cleaning, the saucepan was once more filled and set on the fire, but with no better success. The milk was hopelessly spoilt, and the housewife shed tears of vexation at the waste, crying, "Never before did such a thing befall me since I kept house! Three quarts of new milk burnt for one meal!"

"And that's sixpence," cried the voice from the chimney. "You didn't save the tinkering after all Mother!"

With which the Hillman himself came tumbling down the chimney, and went off laughing through the door.

But thenceforward the saucepan was as good as any other.

## THE NECK.: a legend of a lake.

On a certain lake there once lived a Neck, or Water Sprite, who desired, above all things, to obtain a human soul. Now when the sun shone this Neck rose up and sat upon the waves and played upon his harp. And he played so sweetly that the winds stayed to listen to him, and the sun lingered in his setting, and the moon rose before her time. And the strain was in praise of immortality.

Furthermore, out of the lake there rose a great rock, whereon dwelt an aged hermit, who by reason of his loneliness was afflicted with a spirit of melancholy; so that when the fit was on him, he was constantly tempted to throw himself into the water, for his life was burdensome to him. But one day, when this gloomy madness had driven him to the edge of the rock to cast himself down, the Neck rose at the same moment, and sitting upon a wave, began to play. And the strain was in praise of immortality. And the melody went straight to the heart of the hermit as a sunbeam goes into a dark cave, and it dispelled his gloom, and he thought all to be as well with him as before it had seemed ill. And he called to the Neck and said, "What is that which thou dost play, my son?"

And the Neck answered, "It is in praise of immortality."

Then said the hermit, "I beg that thou wilt play frequently beneath this rock; for I am an aged and solitary man, and by reason of my loneliness, life becomes a burden to me, and I am tempted to throw it away. But by this gracious strain the evil has been dispelled. Wherefore I beg thee to come often and to play as long as is convenient. And yet I cannot offer thee any reward, for I am poor and without possessions."

Then the Neck replied, "There are treasures below the water as above, and I desire no earthly riches. But if thou canst tell me how I may gain a human soul, I will play on till thou shalt bid me cease."

And the hermit said, "I must consider the matter. But I will return to-morrow at this time and answer thee."

Then the next day he returned as he had said, and the Neck was waiting impatiently on the lake, and he cried, "What news, my father?"

And the hermit said, "If that at any time some human being will freely give his life for thee, thou wilt gain a human soul. But thou also must die the selfsame day."

"The short life for the long one!" cried the Neck; and he played a melody so full of happiness that the blood danced through the hermit's veins as if he were a boy again. But the next day when he came as usual the Neck called to him and said, "My father, I have been thinking. Thou art aged and feeble, and at the most there are but few days of life remaining to thee. Moreover, by reason of thy loneliness even these are a burden. Surely there is none more fit than thou to be the means of procuring me a human soul. Wherefore I beg of thee, let us die to-day."

But the hermit cried out angrily, "Wretch! Is this thy gratitude? Wouldst thou murder me?"

"Nay, old man," replied the Neck, "thou shalt part easily with thy little fag-end of life. I can play upon my harp a strain of such surpassing sadness that no human heart that hears it but must break. And yet the pain of that heartbreak shall be such that thou wilt not know it from rapture. Moreover, when the sun sets below the water, my spirit also will depart without suffering. Wherefore I beg of thee, let us die to-day."

"Truly," said the hermit, "it is because thou art only a Neck, and nothing better, that thou dost not know the value of human life."

"And art thou a man, possessed already of a soul, and destined for immortality," cried the Neck, "and dost haggle and grudge to benefit me by the sacrifice of a few uncertain days, when it is but to exchange them for the life that knows no end?"

"Our days are always uncertain," replied the hermit; "but existence is very sweet, even to the most wretched. Moreover, I see not that thou hast any claim upon mine." Saying which he returned to his cell, but the Neck, flinging aside his harp, sat upon the water, and wept bitterly.

Days passed, and the hermit did not show himself, and at last the Neck resolved to go and visit him. So he took his harp, and taking also the form of a boy with long fair hair and a crimson cap, he appeared in the hermit's cell. There he found the old man stretched upon his pallet, for lie was dying. When he saw the Neck he was glad, and said, "I have desired to see thee, for I repent myself that I did not according to thy wishes. Yet is the desire of life stronger in the human breast than thou canst understand. Nevertheless I am sorry, and I am sorry also that, as I am sick unto death, my life will no longer avail thee. But when I am dead, do thou take all that belongs to me, and dress thyself in my robe, and go out into the world, and do works of mercy, and perchance some one whom thou hast benefited will be found willing to die with thee, that thou mayst obtain a soul."

"Now indeed I thank thee!" cried the Neck. "But yet one word more—what are these works of which thou speakest?"

"The corporal works of mercy are seven," gasped the hermit, raising himself on his arm. "To feed the hungry and give the thirsty drink, to visit the sick, to redeem captives, to clothe the naked, to shelter the stranger and the houseless, to visit the widow and fatherless, and to bury the dead." Then even as he spoke the last words the hermit died. And the Neck clothed himself in his robe, and, not to delay in following the directions given to him, he buried the hermit with pious care, and planted flowers upon his grave. After which he went forth into the world.

Now for three hundred years did the Neck go about doing acts of mercy and charity towards men. And amongst the hungry, and the naked, and the sick, and the poor, and the captives, there were not a few who seemed to be weary of this life of many sorrows. But when he had fed the hungry, and clothed the naked, and relieved the sick, and made the poor rich, and set the captive free, life was too dear to all of them to be given up. Therefore he betook himself to the most miserable amongst men, and offering nothing but an easy death in a good cause, he hoped to find some aged and want-worn creature who would do him the kindness he desired. But of those who must look forward to the fewest days and to the most misery there was not one but, like the fabled woodcutter, chose to trudge out to the end his miserable span.

So when three hundred years were past, the Neck's heart failed him, and he said, "All this avails nothing. Wherefore I will return to the lake, and there abide what shall befall." And this he accordingly did.

Now one evening there came a tempest down from the hills, and there was a sudden squall on the lake. And a certain young man in a boat upon the lake was overtaken by the storm. And as he struggled hard, and it seemed as if every moment must be his last, a young maid who was his sweetheart came down to the shore, and cried aloud in her agony, "Alas, that his young life should be cut short thus!"

"Trouble not thyself," said the Neck; "this life is so short and so uncertain, that if he were rescued to-day he might be taken from thee to-morrow. Only in eternity is love secure. Wherefore be patient, and thou shalt soon follow him."

"And who art thou that mockest my sorrow?" cried the maiden.

"One who has watched the passing misfortunes of many generations before thine," replied the Neck.

And when the maiden looked, and saw one like a little old man wringing out his beard into the lake, she knew it was a Neck, and cried, "Now surely thou art a Neck, and they say, 'When Necks play, the winds wisht:' wherefore I beg of thee to play upon thy harp, and it may be that the storm will lull, and my beloved will be saved."

But the Neck answered, "It is not worth while."

And when the maiden could not persuade him, she fell upon her face in bitter grief, and cried, "Oh, my Beloved! Would GOD I could die for thee!"

"And yet thou wouldst not if thou couldst," said the Neck.

"If it be in thy power to prove me—prove me!" cried the maiden; "for indeed he is the only stay of aged parents, and he is young and unprepared for death. Moreover his life is dearer to me than my own."

Then the Neck related his own story, and said, "If thou wilt do this for me, which none yet has done whom I have benefited, I will play upon my harp, and if the winds wisht, thou must die this easy death; but if I fail in my part, I shall not expect thine to be fulfilled. And we must both abide what shall befall, even as others." And to this the maiden consented most willingly. Only she said, "Do this for me, I beg of thee. Let him come so near that I may just see his face before I die." And it was so agreed.

Then the aged Neck drew forth his harp and began to play. And as he played the wind stayed, as one who pauses to hearken with cleft lips, and the lake rose and fell gently, like the bosom of a girl moved by some plaintive song, and the sun burst forth as if to see who made such sweet music. And so through this happy change the young man got safe to land. Then the Neck turned to the maiden and said, "Dost thou hold to thy promise?" And she bowed her head.

"In the long life be thy recompense!" cried the Neck, fervently, and taking his harp again, he poured his whole spirit into the strain. And as he played, it seemed as if the night wind moaned among pine-trees, but it was more mournful. And it was as the wail of a mother for her only son, and yet fuller of grief. Or like a Dead March wrung from the heart of a great musician—loading the air with sorrow—and yet all these were as nothing to it for sadness. And when the maiden heard it, it was more than she could bear, and her heart broke, as the Neck had said. Then the young man sprang to shore, and when she could see his face clearly, her soul passed, and her body fell like a snapped flower to the earth.

Now when the young man knew what was befallen, he fell upon the Neck to kill him, who said, "Thou mayest spare thyself this trouble, for in a few moments I shall be dead. But do thou take my robe and my harp, and thou shalt be a famous musician."

Now even as the Neck spoke the sun sank, and he fell upon his face. And when the young man lifted the robe, behold there was nothing under it but the harp, across which there swept such a wild and piteous chord that all the strings burst as if with unutterable grief.

Then the young man lifted the body of his sweetheart in his arms, and carried her home, and she was buried with many tears.

And in due time he put fresh strings to the harp, which, though it was not as when it was in the hands of the Neck, yet it made most exquisite music. And the young man became a famous musician. For out of suffering comes song.

Furthermore, he occupied himself in good works until that his time also came.

And in Eternity Love was made secure.

## THE NIX IN MISCHIEF.

A certain lake in Germany was once the home of a Nix, who became tired of the monotony of life under water, and wished to go into the upper world and amuse himself.

His friends and relations all tried to dissuade him. "Be wise," said they, "and remain where you are safe, seeing that no business summons you from the lake. Few of our kindred have had dealings with the human race without suffering from their curiosity or clumsiness; and, do them what good you may, in the long run you will reap nothing but ingratitude. From how many waters have they not already banished us? Wherefore let well alone, and stay where you are."

But this counsel did not please the Nix—(as, indeed, there is no reason to suppose that advice is more palatable under water than on dry land)—and he only said, "I shall not expect gratitude, for I have no intention of conferring benefits; but I wish to amuse myself. The Dwarfs and Kobolds play what pranks they please on men and women, and they do not always have the worst of it. When I hear of their adventures, the soles of my feet tingle. This is a sign of travelling, and am I to be debarred from fun because I live in a lake instead of a hill?"

His friends repeated their warnings, but to no purpose. The Nix remained unconvinced, and spent his time in dreaming of the clever tricks by which he should outwit the human race, and the fame he would thereby acquire on his return to the lake.

Mischief seldom lacks opportunity, and shortly after this it happened that a young girl came down to the lake for water to wash with; and dipping her pail just above the Nix's head, in a moment he jumped in, and was brought safe to land. The maid was Bess, the washerwoman's daughter; and as she had had one good scolding that morning for oversleeping herself, and another about noon for dawdling with her work, she took up the pail and set off home without delay.

But though she held it steadily enough, the bucket shook, and the water spilled hither and thither. Thinking that her right arm might be tired, she moved the weight to her left, but with no better success, for the water still spilled at every step. "One would think there were fishes in the pail," said Bess, as she set it down. But there was nothing to be seen but a thin red water-worm wriggling at the bottom, such as you may see any day in a soft-water tub. It was in this shape, however, that the Nix had disguised himself, and he almost writhed out of his skin with delight at the success of his first essay in mischief.

When they once more set forward the Nix leaped and jumped harder than ever, so that not only was the water spilled, but the maiden's dress was soaked, and her tears dropped almost as fast as the wet dripped from her clothes.

"The pail is bewitched!" cried the poor girl. "How my mother will beat me for this! And my back aches as if I were carrying lead, and yet the water is nearly all gone."

"This is something like fun!" laughed the Nix. "When I go home and relate my adventures, no dwarfs pranks will be named again!" But when Bess looked into the pail, he was the same slimy, stupid-looking worm as before. She dared not return to the lake for more water—"for," said she, "I should be as much beaten for being late as for bringing short measure, and have the labour to boot." So she took up her burden again, and the Nix began his dance afresh, and by the time they came to their journey's end, there was not a quart of water in the pail.

"Was ever a poor woman plagued with such a careless hussy?" cried the mother when she saw the dripping dress; and, as Bess had expected, she seasoned her complaints with a hearty slap. "And look what she calls a pailful of water!" added the mother, with a second blow.

"Late in the morning's unlucky all day," thought poor Bess, and, as her mother curled her, she screamed till the house rang with the noise; for she had good lungs, and knew that it is well to cry out before one gets too much hurt.

Meanwhile the Nix thought she was enduring agonies, and could hardly contain his mischievous glee; and when the woman bade her "warm some water quickly for the wash," he was in no way disturbed, for he had never seen boiling water, and only anticipated fresh sport as he slipped from the pail into the kettle.

"Now," cried the mother sharply, "see if you can lift that without slopping your clothes."

"Aye, aye," laughed the Nix, "see if you can, my dear!" and as poor Bess seized it in her sturdy red hands he began to dance as before. But the kettle had a lid, which the pail had not. Moreover Bess was a strong, strapping lass, and, stimulated by the remembrance of her mother's slaps, with a vigorous effort she set the kettle on the fire. "I shall be glad when I'm safely in bed," she muttered. "Everything goes wrong to-day."

"It is warm in here," said the Nix to himself, after a while; "in fact—stuffy. But one must pay something for a frolic, and it tickles my ears to hear that old woman rating her daughter for my pranks. Give me time and opportunity, and I'll set the whole stupid race by the ears. There she goes again! It is worth enduring a little discomfort, though it certainly is warm, and I fancy it grows warmer."

By degrees the bottom of the kettle grew quite hot, and burnt the Nix, so that he had to jump up and down in the water to keep himself cool. The noise of this made the woman think that the kettle was boiling, and she began to scold her daughter as before, shouting, "Are you coming with that tub to-night or not? The water is hot already."

This time the Nix laughed (as they say) on the other side of his mouth; for the water had now become as hot as the bottom of the kettle, and he screamed at the top of his shrill tiny voice with pain.

"How the kettle sings to-night!" said Bess, "and how it rains!" she added. For at that moment a tremendous storm burst around the house, and the rain poured down in sheets of water, as if it meant to wash everything into the lake. The kettle now really boiled, and the lid danced up and down with the frantic leaping and jumping of the agonized Nix, who puffed and blew till his breath came out of the spout in clouds of steam.

"If your eyes were as sharp as your ears you'd see that the water is boiling over," snapped the woman; and giving her daughter a passing push, she hurried to the fire-place, and lifted the kettle on to the ground.

But no sooner had she set it down, than the lid flew off, and out jumped a little man with green teeth and a tall green hat, who ran out of the door wringing his hands and crying—

"Three hundred and three years have I lived in the water of this lake, and I never knew it boil before!"

As he crossed the threshold, a clap of thunder broke with what sounded like a peal of laughter from many voices, and then the storm ceased as suddenly as it had begun.

The woman now saw how matters stood, and did not fail next morning to fasten an old horseshoe to the door of her house. And seeing that she had behaved unjustly to her daughter, she bought her the gayest set of pink ribbons that were to be found at the next fair.

It is on record that Bess (who cared little for slaps and sharp speeches) thought this the best bargain she had ever made. But whether the Nix was equally well satisfied is not known.

## THE COBBLER AND THE GHOSTS.

Long ago there lived a cobbler who had very poor wits, but by strict industry he could earn enough to keep himself and his widowed mother in comfort.

In this manner he had lived for many years in peace and prosperity, when a distant relative died who left him a certain sum of money. This so elated the cobbler that he could think of nothing else, and his only talk was of the best way of spending the legacy.

His mother advised him to lay it by against a rainy day.

"For," said she, "we have lived long in much comfort as we are, and have need of nothing; but when you grow old, or if it should please Heaven that you become disabled, you will then be glad of your savings."

But to this the cobbler would not listen. "No," said he, "if we save the money it may be stolen, but if we spend it well, we shall have the use of what we buy, and may sell it again if we are so minded."

He then proposed one purchase after another, and each was more foolish than the rest. When this had gone on for some time, one morning he exclaimed: "I have it at last! We will buy the house. It cannot be stolen or lost, and when it is ours we shall have no rent to pay, and I shall not have to work so hard."

"He will never hit on a wiser plan than that," thought the widow; "it is not to be expected." So she fully consented to this arrangement, which was duly carried out; and the bargain left the cobbler with a few shillings, which he tied up in a bag and put in his pocket, having first changed them into pence, that they might make more noise when he jingled the bag as he walked down the street.

Presently he said; "It is not fit that a man who lives in his own house, and has ready money in his pocket too, should spend the whole day in labouring with his hands. Since by good luck I can read, it would be well that I should borrow a book from the professor, for study is an occupation suitable to my present position."

Accordingly, he went to the professor, whom he found seated in his library, and preferred his request.

"What book do you want?" asked the professor.

The cobbler stood and scratched his head thoughtfully. The professor thought that he was trying to recall the name of the work; but in reality he was saying to himself: "How much additional knowledge one requires if he has risen ever so little in life! Now, if I did but know where it is proper to begin in a case full of books like this! Should one take the first on the top shelf, or the bottom shelf, to the left, or to the right?"

At last he resolved to choose the book nearest to him; so drawing it out from the rest, he answered—

"This one, if it please you, learned sir." The professor lent it to him, and he took it home and began to read.

It was, as it happened, a book about ghosts and apparitions; and the cobbler's mind was soon so full of these marvels that he could talk of nothing else, and hardly did a stroke of work for reading and pondering over what he read. He could find none of his neighbours who had seen a ghost, though most had heard of such things, and many believed in them.

"Live and learn," thought the cobbler; "here is fame as well as wealth. If I could but see a ghost there would be no more to desire." And with this intent he sallied forth late one night to the churchyard.

Meanwhile a thief (who had heard the jingle of his money-bag) resolved to profit by the cobbler's whim; so wrapping himself in a sheet, he laid wait for him in a field that he must cross to reach the church.

When the cobbler saw the white figure, he made sure, that he had now seen a ghost, and already felt proud of his own acquaintance, as a remarkable character. Meanwhile, the thief stood quite still, and the cobbler walked boldly up to him, expecting that the phantom would either vanish or prove so impalpable that he could pass through it as through a mist, of which he had read many notable instances in the professor's book. He soon found out his mistake, however, for the supposed ghost grappled him, and without loss of time relieved him of his money-bag. The cobbler (who was not wanting in courage) fastened as tightly on to the sheet, which he still held with desperate firmness when the thief had slipped through his fingers; and after waiting in vain for further marvels, he carried the sheet home to his mother, and narrated his encounter with the ghost.

"Alack-a-day! that I should have a son with so little wit!" cried the old woman; "it was no ghost, but a thief, who is now making merry with all the money we possessed."

"We have his sheet," replied her son; "and that is due solely to my determination. How could I have acted better?"

"You should have grasped the man, not the sheet," said the widow, "and pummelled him till he cried out and dropped the money-bag."

"Live and learn," said the cobbler. The next night he went out as before, and this time reached the churchyard unmolested. He was just climbing the stile, when he again saw what seemed to be a white figure standing near the church. As before, it proved solid, and this time he pummelled it till his fingers bled, and for very weariness he was obliged to go home and relate his exploits. The ghost had not cried out, however, nor even so much as moved, for it was neither more nor less than a tall tombstone shining white in the moonlight.

"Alack-a-day!" cried the old woman, "that I should have a son with so little wit as to beat a gravestone till his knuckles are sore! Now if he had covered it with something black that it might not alarm timid women or children, that would at least have been an act of charity."

"Live and learn," said the cobbler. The following night he again set forth, but this time in another direction. As he was crossing a field behind his house he saw some long pieces of linen which his mother had put out to bleach in the dew.

"More ghosts!" cried the shoemaker, "and they know who is behind them. They have fallen flat at the sound of my footsteps. But one must think of others as well as oneself, and it is not every heart that is as stout as mine." Saying which he returned to the house for something black to throw over the prostrate ghosts. Now the kitchen chimney had been swept that morning, and by the back door stood a sack of soot.

"What is blacker than soot?" said the cobbler; and taking the sack, he shook it out over the pieces of linen till not a thread of white was to be seen. After which he went home, and boasted of his good deeds.

The widow now saw that she must be more careful as to what she said; so, after weighing the matter for some time, she suggested to the cobbler that the next night he should watch for ghosts at home; "for they are to be seen," said she, "as well when one is in bed as in the fields."

"There you are right," said the cobbler, "for I have this day read of a ghost that appeared to a man in his own house. The candles burnt blue, and when he had called thrice upon the apparition, he became senseless."

"That was his mistake," said the old woman. "He should have turned a deaf ear, and even pretended to slumber; but it is not every one who has courage for this. If one could really fall asleep in the face of the apparition, there would be true bravery."

"Leave that to me," said the cobbler. And the widow went off chuckling, to herself, "If he comes to any mischance by holding his tongue and going to sleep, ill-luck has got him by the leg, and counsel is wasted on him."

As soon as his mother was in bed, the cobbler prepared for his watch. First he got together all the candles in the house, and stuck them here and there about the kitchen, and sat down to watch till they should burn blue. After waiting some time, during which the candles only guttered with the draughts, the cobbler decided to go to rest for a while. "It is too early yet," he thought; "I shall see nothing till midnight."

Very soon, however, he fell asleep; but towards morning he awoke, and in the dim light perceived a figure in white at his bedside. It was a blacksmith who lived near, and he had run in in his night-shirt without so much as slippers on his feet.

"The ghost at last!" thought the cobbler, and, remembering his mother's advice, he turned over and shut his eyes.

"Neighbour! neighbour!" cried the blacksmith, "your house is on fire!"

"An old bird is not to be caught with chaff," chuckled the cobbler to himself; and he pulled the bed-clothes over his head.

"Neighbour!" roared the blacksmith, snatching at the quilt to drag it off, "are you mad? The house is burning over your head. Get up for your life!"

"I have the courage of a general, and more," thought the cobbler; and holding tightly on to the clothes he pretended to snore.

"If you will burn, burn!" cried the blacksmith angrily, "but I mean to save my bones"—with which he ran off.

And burnt the cobbler undoubtedly would have been, had not his mother's cries at last convinced him that the candles had set fire to his house, which was wrapped in flames. With some difficulty he escaped with his life, but of all he possessed nothing remained to him but his tools and a few articles of furniture that the widow had saved.

As he was now again reduced to poverty, he was obliged to work as diligently as in former years, and passed the rest of his days in the same peace and prosperity which he had before enjoyed.

# THE LAIRD AND THE MAN OF PEACE.

In the Highlands of Scotland there once lived a Laird of Brockburn, who would not believe in fairies. Although his sixth cousin on the mother's side, as he returned one night from a wedding, had seen the Men of Peace hunting on the sides of Ben Muich Dhui, dressed in green, and with silver-mounted bridles to their horses which jingled as they rode; and though Rory the fiddler having gone to play at a christening did never come home, but crossing a hill near Brockburn in a mist was seduced into a Shian or fairy turret, where, as all decent bodies well believe, he is playing still—in spite, I say, of the wise saws and experience of all his neighbours, Brockburn remained obstinately incredulous.

Not that he bore any ill-will to the Good People, or spoke uncivilly of them; indeed he always disavowed any feeling of disrespect towards them if they existed, saying that he was a man of peace himself, and anxious to live peaceably with whatever neighbours he had, but that till he had seen one of the Daoiné Shi he could not believe in them.

Now one afternoon, between Hallowmas and Yule, it chanced that the Laird, being out on the hills looking for some cattle, got parted from his men and dogs and was overtaken by a mist, in which, familiar as the country was to him, he lost his way.

In vain he raised his voice high, and listened low, no sound of man or beast came back to him through the thickening vapour.

Then night fell, and darkness was added to the fog, so that Brockburn needed to sound every step with his rung before he took it.

Suddenly light footsteps pattered beside him, then Something rubbed against him, then It ran between his legs. The delighted Laird made sure that his favourite collie had found him once more.

"Wow, Jock, man!" he cried; "but ye needna throw me on my face. What's got ye the night, that you should lose your way in a bit mist?"

To this a voice from the level of his elbow replied, in piping but patronizing tones;

"Never did I lose my way in a mist since the night that Finn crossed over to Ireland in the Dawn of History. Eh, Laird! I'm weel acquaint with every bit path on the hill-side these hundreds of years, and I'll guide ye safe hame, never fear!"

The hairs on Brockburn's head stood on end till they lifted his broad bonnet, and a damp chill broke out over him that was not the fog. But, for all that, he stoutly resisted the evidence of his senses, and only felt about him for the collie's head to pat, crying:

"Bark! Jock, my mannie, bark! Then I'll recognize your voice, ye ken. It's no canny to hear ye speak like a Christian, my wee doggie."

"I'm nae your doggie, I'm a Man of Peace," was the reply. "Dinna miscall your betters, Brockburn: why will ye not credit our existence, man?"

"Seein's believin'," said the Laird, stubbornly; "but the mist's ower thick for seein' the night, ye ken."

"Turn roun' to your left, man, and ye'll see," said the Dwarf, and catching Brockburn by the arm, he twisted him swiftly round three times, when a sudden blaze of light poured through the mist, and revealed a crag of the mountain well known to the Laird, and which he now saw to be a kind of turret, or tower.

Lights shone gaily through the crevices or windows of the Shian, and sounds of revelry came forth, among which fiddling was conspicuous. The tune played at that moment was "Delvyn-side."

Blinded by the light, and amazed at what he saw, the Laird staggered, and was silent.

"Keep to your feet, man—keep to your feet!" said the Dwarf, laughing. "I doubt ye're fou, Brockburn!"

"I'm nae fou," said the Laird, slowly, his rung grasped firmly in his hand, and his bonnet set back from his face, which was deadly pale. "But—man-is yon Rory? I'd know his fiddle in a thousand."

"Ask no questions, and ye'll be tellt no lees," said the Dwarf. Then stepping up to the door of the Shian, he stood so that the light from within fell full upon him, and the astonished Laird saw a tiny but well-proportioned man, with delicate features, and golden hair flowing over his shoulders. He wore a cloak of green cloth, lined with daisies, and had silver shoes. His beautiful face quivered with amusement, and he cried triumphantly, "D'ye see me?—d'ye see me noo, Brockburn?"

"Aye, aye," said the Laird; "and seein's believin'."

"Then roun' wi' ye!" shouted the Man of Peace; and once more seizing the Laird by the arm, he turned him swiftly round—this time, to the right—and at the third turn the light vanished, and Brockburn and the Man of Peace were once more alone together in the mist.

"Aweel, Brockburn," said the Man of Peace, "I'll alloo ye're candid, and have a convincible mind. I'm no ill disposit to ye, and yese get safe hame, man."

As he spoke he stooped down, and picking up half-a-dozen big stones from the mountain-side, he gave them to the Laird, saying, "If the gudewife asks ye about the bit stanes, say ye got them in a compliment."

Brockburn put them into his pocket, briefly saying, "I'm obleeged to ye;" but as he followed the Man of Peace down the hill-side, he found the obligation so heavy, that from time to time he threw a stone away, unobserved, as he hoped, by his companion. When the first stone fell, the Man of Peace looked sharply round, saying:

"What's yon?"

"It'll be me striking my rung upon the ground," said the Laird.

"You're mad," said the Man of Peace, and Brockburn felt sure that he knew the truth, and was displeased. But as they went on, the stones were so heavy, and bumped the Laird's side so hard, that he threw away a second, dropping it as gently as he could. But the sound of its fall did not escape the ears of the Man of Peace, who cried as before:

"What's yon?"

"It's jest a nasty hoast that I have," said the Laird.

"Man, you're daft," said the Dwarf, contemptuously; "that's what ails ye."

The Laird now resolved to be prudent, but the inconvenience of his burden was so great that after a while he resolved to risk the displeasure of the Man of Peace once more, and gently slipped a third stone to the ground.

"Third time's lucky," he thought. But the proverb failed him, for the Dwarf turned as before, shouting: "What's yon?"

"It'll be my new brogues that ye hear bumpin' Upon the muckle stanes," said the Laird.

"Ye're fou, Brockburn, I tellt ye so. Ye're fou!" growled the Man of Peace, angrily, and the Laird dared not drop any more of the Dwarfs gifts. After a while his companion's good-humour seemed to return, and he became talkative and generous.

"I mind your great-grandfather weel, Brockburn. He was a hamely man, I found his sheep for him one nicht on this verra hill-side. Mair by token, ye'll find your beasties at hame, and the men and the dogs forebye."

The Laird thanked him heartily, and after a while the Dwarf became more liberal-spirited still.

"Yese no have to say that ye've been with the Daoiné Shi and are no the better for it," he said. "I'm thinking I'll grant ye three wushes. But choose wisely, man, and dinna throw them away. I hae my fears that ye're no without a bee in your bonnet, Brockburn."

Incensed by this insinuation, the Laird defended his own sagacity at some length, and retorted on his companion with doubts of the power of the Daoiné Shi to grant wishes.

"The proof of the pudding's in the eating o't," said the Man of Peace. "Wush away, Brockburn, and mak the nut as hard to crack as ye will."

The Laird at once began to cast about in his mind for three wishes sufficiently comprehensive to secure his lifelong prosperity; but the more he beat his brains the less could he satisfy himself.

How many miles he wandered thus, the Dwarf keeping silently beside him, he never knew, before he sank exhausted on the ground, saying:

"I'm thinking, man, that if ye could bring hame to me, in place of bringing me hame, I'd misdoubt your powers nae mair. It's a far cry to Loch Awe, ye ken, and it's a weary long road to Brockburn."

"Is this your wush?" asked the Man of Peace.

"This is my wush," said the Laird, striking his rung upon the ground.

The words had scarcely passed his lips when the whole homestead of Brockburn, house and farm buildings, was planted upon the bleak hill-side.

The astonished Laird now began to bewail the rash wish which had removed his home from the sheltered and fertile valley where it originally stood to the barren side of a bleak mountain.

The Man of Peace, however, would not take any hints as to undoing his work of his own accord. All he said was:

"If ye wush it away, so it'll be. But then ye'll only have one wush left. Ye've small discretion the nicht, Brockburn, I'm feared."

"To leave the steading in sic a spot is no to be thought on," sighed the Laird, as he spent his second wish in undoing his first. But he cannily added the provision:

"And ye may tak me wi' it."

The words were no sooner spoken than the homestead was back in its place, and Brockburn himself was lying in his own bed, Jock, his favourite collie, barking and licking his face by turns for joy.

"Whisht, whisht, Jock!" said the Laird. "Ye wouldna bark when I begged of ye, so ye may hand your peace noo."

And pushing the collie from him, he sat up in bed and looked anxiously but vainly round the chamber for the Man of Peace.

"Lie doun, lie doun," cried the gudewife from beside him. "Ye're surely out o' your wuts, Brockburn. Would ye gang stravaging about the country again the nicht?"

"Where is he?" cried the Laird.

"There's not a soul here but your lawful wife and your ain dear doggie. Was there ae body that ye expected?" asked his wife.

"The Man o' Peace, woman!" cried Brockburn. "I've ane o' my wushes to get, and I maun hae't."

"The man's mad!" was the gudewife's comment. "Ye've surely forgotten yoursel, Brockburn. Ye never believed in the Daoiné Shi before."

"Seein's believin'," said the Laird. "I forgathered with a Man o' Peace the nicht on the hill, and I wush I just saw him again."

As the Laird spoke the window of the chamber was lit up from without, and the Man of Peace appeared sitting on the window-ledge in his daisy-lined cloak, his feet hanging down into the room, the silver shoes glittering as they dangled.

"I'm here, Brockburn!" he cried. "But eh, man! ye've had your last wush."

And even as the stupefied Laird gazed, the light slowly died away, and the Man of Peace vanished also.

On the following morning the Laird was roused from sleep by loud cries of surprise and admiration.

The good wife had been stirring for some hours, and in emptying the pockets of her good man's coat she had found three huge cairngorms of exquisite tint and lustre. Brockburn thus discovered the value of the gifts, half of which he had thrown away.

But no subsequent visits to the hill-side led to their recovery. Many a time did the Laird bring home a heavy pocketful of stones, at the thrifty gude-wife's bidding, but they only proved to be the common stones of the mountain-side. The Shian could never be distinguished from any other crag, and the Daoiné Shi were visible no more.

Yet it is said that the Laird of Brockburn prospered and throve thereafter, in acre, stall, and steading, as those seldom prosper who have not the good word of the People of Peace.

# THE OGRE COURTING.

In days when ogres were still the terror of certain districts, there was one who had long kept a whole neighbourhood in fear without any one daring to dispute his tyranny.

By thefts and exactions, by heavy ransoms from merchants too old and tough to be eaten, in one way and another, the Ogre had become very rich; and although those who knew could tell of huge cellars full of gold and jewels, and yards and barns groaning with the weight of stolen goods, the richer he grew the more anxious and covetous he became. Moreover, day by day, he added to his stores; for though (like most ogres) he was as stupid as he was strong, no one had ever been found, by force or fraud, to get the better of him.

What he took from the people was not their heaviest grievance. Even to be killed and eaten by him was not the chance they thought of most. A man can die but once; and if he is a sailor, a shark may eat him, which is not so much better than being devoured by an ogre. No, that was not the worst. The worst was this—he would keep getting married. And as he liked little wives, all the short women lived in fear and dread. And as his wives always died very soon, he was constantly courting fresh ones.

Some said he ate his wives; some said he tormented, and others, that he only worked them to death. Everybody knew it was not a desirable match, and yet there was not a father who dare refuse his daughter if she were asked for. The Ogre only cared for two things in a woman—he liked her to be little, and a good housewife.

Now it was when the Ogre had just lost his twenty-fourth wife (within the memory of man) that these two qualities were eminently united in the person of the smallest and most notable woman of the district, the daughter of a certain poor farmer. He was so poor that he could not afford properly to dower his daughter, who had in consequence remained single beyond her first youth. Everybody felt sure that Managing Molly must now be married to the Ogre. The tall girls stretched themselves till they looked like maypoles, and said, "Poor thing!" The slatterns gossiped from house to house, the heels of their shoes clacking as they went, and cried that this was what came of being too thrifty.

And sure enough, in due time, the giant widower came to the farmer as he was in the field looking over his crops, and proposed for Molly there and then. The farmer was so much put out that he did not know what he said in reply, either when he was saying it, or afterwards, when his friends asked about it. But he remembered that the Ogre had invited himself to sup at the farm that day week.

Managing Molly did not distress herself at the news.

"Do what I bid you, and say as I say," said she to her father, "and if the Ogre does not change his mind, at any rate you shall not come empty-handed out of the business."

By his daughter's desire the farmer now procured a large number of hares, and a barrel of white wine, which expenses completely emptied his slender stocking, and on the day of the Ogre's visit, she made a delicious and savoury stew with the hares in the biggest pickling tub, and the wine-barrel was set on a bench near the table.

When the Ogre came, Molly served up the stew, and the Ogre sat down to sup, his head just touching the kitchen rafters. The stew was perfect, and there was plenty of it. For what Molly and her father ate was hardly to be counted in the tubful. The Ogre was very much pleased, and said politely:

"I'm afraid, my dear, that you have been put to great trouble and expense on my account, I have a large appetite, and like to sup well."

"Don't mention it, sir," said Molly. "The fewer rats the more corn. How do you cook them?"

"Not one of all the extravagant hussies I have had as wives ever cooked them at all," said the Ogre; and he thought to himself, "Such a stew out of rats! What frugality! What a housewife!"

When he broached the wine, he was no less pleased, for it was of the best.

"This, at any rate, must have cost you a great deal, neighbour," said he, drinking the farmer's health as Molly left the room.

"I don't know that rotten apples could be better used," said the farmer; "but I leave all that to Molly. Do you brew at home?"

"We give our rotten apples to the pigs," growled the Ogre. "But things will be better ordered when she is my wife."

The Ogre was now in great haste to conclude the match, and asked what dowry the farmer would give his daughter.

"I should never dream of giving a dowry with Molly," said the farmer, boldly. "Whoever gets her, gets dowry enough. On the contrary, I shall expect a good round sum from the man who deprives me of her. Our wealthiest farmer is just widowed, and therefore sure to be in a hurry for marriage. He has an eye to the main chance, and would not grudge to pay well for such a wife, I'll warrant."

"I'm no churl myself," said the Ogre, who was anxious to secure his thrifty bride at any price; and he named a large sum of money, thinking, "We shall live on rats henceforward, and the beef and mutton will soon cover the dowry."

"Double that, and we'll see," said the farmer, stoutly.

But the Ogre became angry, and cried; "What are you thinking of, man? Who is to hinder my carrying your lass off, without 'with your leave' or 'by your leave,' dowry or none?"

"How little you know her!" said the farmer. "She is so firm that she would be cut to pieces sooner than give you any benefit of her thrift, unless you dealt fairly in the matter."

"Well, well," said the Ogre, "let us meet each other." And he named a sum larger than he at first proposed, and less than the farmer had asked. This the farmer agreed to, as it was enough to make him prosperous for life.

"Bring it in a sack to-morrow morning," said he to the Ogre, "and then you can speak to Molly; she's gone to bed now."

The next morning, accordingly, the Ogre appeared, carrying the dowry in a sack, and Molly came to meet him.

"There are two things," said she, "I would ask of any lover of mine: a new farmhouse, built as I should direct, with a view to economy; and a feather-bed of fresh goose feathers, filled when the old woman plucks her geese. If I don't sleep well, I cannot work well."

"That is better than asking for finery," thought the Ogre; "and after all the house will be my own." So, to save the expense of labour, he built it himself, and worked hard, day after day, under Molly's orders, till winter came. Then it was finished.

"Now for the feather-bed," said Molly. "I'll sew up the ticking, and when the old woman plucks her geese, I'll let you know."

When it snows, they say the old woman up yonder is plucking her geese, and so at the first snowstorm Molly sent for the Ogre.

"Now you see the feathers falling," said she, "so fill the bed."

"How am I to catch them?" cried the Ogre.

"Stupid! don't you see them lying there in a heap?" cried Molly; "get a shovel, and set to work."

The Ogre accordingly carried in shovelfuls of snow to the bed, but as it melted as fast as he put it in, his labour never seemed done. Towards night the room got so cold that the snow would not melt, and now the bed was soon filled.

Molly hastily covered it with sheets and blankets, and said: "Pray rest here to-night, and tell me if the bed is not comfort itself. To-morrow we will be married."

So the tired Ogre lay down on the bed he had filled, but, do what he would, he could not get warm.

"The sheets must be damp," said he, and in the morning he woke with such horrible pains in his bones that he could hardly move, and half the bed had melted away. "It's no use," he groaned, "she's a very managing woman, but to sleep on such a bed would be the death of me." And he went off home as quickly as he could, before Managing Molly could call upon him to be married; for she was so managing that he was more than half afraid of her already.

When Molly found that he had gone, she sent the farmer after him.

"What does he want?" cried the Ogre, when they told him the farmer was at the door.

"He says the bride is waiting for you," was the reply.

"Tell him I'm too ill to be married," said the Ogre.

But the messenger soon returned:

"He says she wants to know what you will give her to make up for the disappointment."

"She's got the dowry, and the farm, and the feather-bed," groaned the Ogre; "what more does she want?"

But again the messenger returned:

"She says you've pressed the feather-bed flat, and she wants some more goose feathers."

"There are geese enough in the yard," yelled the Ogre, "Let him drive them home; and if he has another word to say, put him down to roast."

The farmer, who overheard this order, lost no time in taking his leave, and as he passed through the yard he drove home as fine a flock of geese as you will see on a common.

It is said that the Ogre never recovered from the effects of sleeping on the old woman's goose feathers, and was less powerful than before.

As for Managing Molly, being now well dowered, she had no lack of offers of marriage, and was soon mated to her mind.

## THE MAGICIANS' GIFTS.

There was once a king in whose dominions lived no less than three magicians.

When the king's eldest son was christened, the king invited the three magicians to the christening feast, and to make the compliment the greater, he asked one of them to stand godfather. But the other two, who were not asked to be godfathers, were so angry at what they held to be a slight, that they only waited to see how they might best revenge themselves upon the infant prince.

When the moment came for presenting the christening gifts, the godfather magician advanced to the cradle and said, "My gift is this: Whatever he wishes for he shall have. And only I who give shall be able to recall this gift." For he perceived the jealousy of the other magicians, and knew that, if possible, they would undo what he did. But the second magician muttered in his beard, "And yet I will change it to a curse." And coming up to the cradle, he said, "The wishes that he has thus obtained he shall not be able to revoke or change."

Then the third magician grumbled beneath his black robe, "If he were very wise and prudent he might yet be happy. But I will secure his punishment." So he also drew near to the cradle, and said, "For my part, I give him a hasty temper."

After which, the two dissatisfied magicians withdrew together, saying, "Should we permit ourselves to be slighted for nothing?"

But the king and his courtiers were not at all disturbed.

"My son has only to be sure of what he wants," said the king, "and then, I suppose, he will not desire to recall his wishes."

And the courtiers added, "If a prince may not have a hasty temper, who may, we should like to know?"

And everybody laughed, except the godfather magician, who went out sighing and shaking his head, and was seen no more.

Whilst the king's son was yet a child, the gift of the godfather magician began to take effect. There was nothing so rare and precious that he could not obtain it, or so difficult that it could not be accomplished by his mere wish. But, on the other hand, no matter how inconsiderately he spoke, or how often he changed his mind, what he had once wished must remain as he had wished it, in spite of himself; and as he often wished for things that were bad for him, and oftener still wished for a thing one day and regretted it the next, his power was the source of quite as much pain as pleasure to him. Then his temper was so hot, that he was apt hastily to wish ill to those who offended him, and afterwards bitterly to regret the mischief that he could not undo. Thus, one after another, the king appointed his trustiest counsellors to the charge of his son, who, sooner or later, in the discharge of their duty, were sure to be obliged to thwart him; on which the impatient prince would cry, "I wish you were at the bottom of the sea with your rules and regulations;" and the counsellors disappeared accordingly, and returned no more.

When there was not a wise man left at court, and the king himself lived in daily dread of being the next victim, he said, "Only one thing remains to be done: to find the godfather magician, and persuade him to withdraw his gift."

So the king offered rewards, and sent out messengers in every direction, but the magician was not to be found. At last, one day he met a blind beggar, who said to him, "Three nights ago I dreamed that I went by the narrowest of seven roads to seek what you are looking for, and was successful."

When the king returned home, he asked his courtiers, "Where are there seven roads lying near to each other, some broad, and some narrow?" And one of them replied, "Twenty-one miles to the west of the palace is a four-cross road, where three field-paths also diverge."

To this place the king made his way, and taking the narrowest of the field-paths, went on and on till it led him straight into a cave, where an old woman sat over a fire.

"Does a magician live here?" asked the king.

"No one lives here but myself," said the old woman. "But as I am a wise woman I may be able to help you if you need it."

The king then told her of his perplexities, and how he was desirous of finding the magician, to persuade him to recall his gift.

"He could not recall the other gifts," said the wise woman. "Therefore it is better that the prince should be taught to use his power prudently and to control his temper. And since all the persons capable of guiding him have disappeared, I will return with you and take charge of him myself. Over me he will have no power."

To this the king consented, and they returned together to the palace, where the wise woman became guardian to the prince, and she fulfilled her duties so well that he became much more discreet and self-controlled. Only at times his violent temper got the better of him, and led him to wish what he afterwards vainly regretted.

Thus all went well till the prince became a man, when, though he had great affection for her, he felt ashamed of having an old woman for his counsellor, and he said, "I certainly wish that I had a faithful and discreet adviser of my own age and sex."

On that very day a young nobleman offered himself as companion to the prince, and as he was a young man of great ability, he was accepted: whereupon the old woman took her departure, and was never seen again.

The young nobleman performed his part so well that the prince became deeply attached to him, and submitted in every way to his counsels. But at last a day came when, being in a rage, the advice of his friend irritated him, and he cried hastily, "Will you drive me mad with your long sermons? I wish you would hold your tongue for ever." On which the young nobleman became dumb, and so remained. For he was not, as the wise woman had been, independent of the prince's power.

The prince's grief and remorse knew no bounds. "Am I not under a curse?" said he. "Truly I ought to be cast out from human society, and sent to live with wild beasts in a wilderness. I only bring evil upon those I love best—indeed, there is no hope for me unless I can find my godfather, and make him recall this fatal gift."

So the prince mounted his horse, and, accompanied by his dumb friend, who still remained faithful to him, he set forth to find the magician. They took no followers, except the prince's dog, a noble hound, who was so quick of hearing that he understood all that was said to him, and was, next to the young nobleman, the wisest person at court.

"Mark well, my dog," said the prince to him, "we stay nowhere till we find my godfather, and when we find him we go no further. I rely on your sagacity to help us."

The dog licked the prince's hand, and then trotted so resolutely down a certain road that the two friends allowed him to lead them and followed close behind.

They travelled in this way to the edge of the king's dominions, only halting for needful rest and refreshment. At last the dog led them through a wood, and towards evening they found themselves in the depths of the forest, with no sign of any shelter for the night. Presently they heard a little bell, such as is rung for prayer, and the dog ran down a side path and led them straight to a kind of grotto, at the door of which stood an aged hermit.

"Does a magician live here?" asked the prince.

"No one lives here but myself," said the hermit, "but I am old, and have meditated much. My advice is at your service if you need it."

The prince then related his history, and how he was now seeking the magician godfather, to rid himself of his gift.

"And yet that will not cure your temper," said the hermit. "It were better that you employed yourself in learning to control that, and to use your power prudently."

"No, no," replied the prince; "I must find the magician."

And when the hermit pressed his advice, he cried, "Provoke me not, good father, or I may be base enough to wish you ill; and the evil I do I cannot undo."

And he departed, followed by his friend, and calling his dog. But the dog seated himself at the hermit's feet, and would not move. Again and again the prince called him, but he only whined and wagged his tail, and refused to move. Coaxing and scolding were both in vain, and when at last the prince tried to drag him off by force, the dog growled.

"Base brute!" cried the prince, flinging him from him in a transport of rage. "How have I been so deceived in you? I wish you were hanged!" And even as he spoke the dog vanished, and as the prince turned his head he saw the poor beast's body dangling from a tree above him. The sight overwhelmed him, and he began bitterly to lament his cruelty.

"Will no one hang me also," he cried, "and rid the world of such a monster?"

"It is easier to die repenting than to live amending," said the hermit; "yet is the latter course the better one. Wherefore abide with me, my son, and learn in solitude those lessons of self-government without which no man is fit to rule others."

"It is impossible," said the prince. "These fits of passion are as a madness that comes upon me, and they are beyond cure. It only remains to find my godfather, that he may make me less baneful to others by taking away the power I abuse." And raising the body of the dog tenderly in his arms, he laid it before him on his horse, and rode away, the dumb nobleman following him.

They now entered the dominions of another king, and in due time arrived at the capital. The prince presented himself to the king, and asked if he had a magician in his kingdom.

"Not to my knowledge," replied the king. "But I have a remarkably wise daughter, and if you want counsel she may be able to help you."

The princess accordingly was sent for, and she was so beautiful, as well as witty, that the prince fell in love with her, and begged the king to give her to him to wife. The king, of course, was unable to refuse what the prince wished, and the wedding was celebrated without delay; and by the advice of his wife the prince placed the body of his faithful dog in a glass coffin, and kept it near him, that he might constantly be reminded of the evil results of giving way to his anger.

For a time all went well. At first the prince never said a harsh word to his wife; but by and by familiarity made him less careful, and one day she said something that offended him, and he fell into a violent rage. As he went storming up and down, the princess wrung her hands, and cried, "Ah, my dear husband, I beg of you to be careful what you say to me. You say you loved your dog, and yet you know where he lies."

"I know that I wish you were with him, with your prating!" cried the prince, in a fury; and the words were scarcely out of his mouth when the princess vanished from his side, and when he ran to the glass coffin, there she lay, pale and lifeless, with her head upon the body of the hound.

The prince was now beside himself with remorse and misery, and when the dumb nobleman made signs that they should pursue their search for the magician, he only cried, "Too late! too late!"

But after a while he said, "I will return to the hermit, and pass the rest of my miserable life in solitude and penance. And you, dear friend, go back to my father."

But the dumb nobleman shook his head, and could not be persuaded to leave the prince. Then they took the glass coffin on their shoulders, and on foot, and weeping as they went, they retraced their steps to the forest.

For some time the prince remained with the hermit, and submitted himself to his direction. Then the hermit bade him return to his father, and he obeyed.

Every day the prince stood by the glass coffin, and beat his breast and cried, "Behold, murderer, the fruits of anger!" And he tried hard to overcome the violence of his temper. When he lost heart he remembered a saying of the hermit: "Patience had far to go, but she was crowned at last." And after a while the prince became as gentle as he had before been violent. And the king and all the court rejoiced at the change; but the prince remained sad at heart, thinking of the princess.

One day he was sitting alone, when a man approached him, dressed in a long black robe.

"Good-day, godson," said he.

"Who calls me godson?" said the prince.

"The magician you have so long sought," said the godfather. "I have come to reclaim my gift."

"What cruelty led you to bestow it upon me?" asked the prince.

"The king, your father, would have been dissatisfied with any ordinary present from me," said the magician, "forgetting that the responsibilities of common gifts, and very limited power, are more than enough for most men to deal with. But I have not neglected you. I was the wise woman who brought you up. Again, I was the hermit, as your dog was sage enough to discover. I am come now to reclaim what has caused you such suffering."

"Alas!" cried the prince, "why is your kindness so tardy? If you have not forgotten me, why have you withheld this benefit till it is too late for my happiness? My friend is dumb, my wife is dead, my dog is hanged. When wishes cannot reach these, do you think it matters to me what I may command?"

"Softly, prince," said the magician; "I had a reason for the delay. But for these bitter lessons you would still be the slave of the violent temper which you have conquered, and which, as it was no gift of mine, I could not remove. Moreover, when the spell which made all things bend to your wish is taken away, its effects also are undone. Godson! I recall my gift."

As the magician spoke the glass sides of the coffin melted into the air, and the princess sprang up, and threw herself into her husband's arms. The dog also rose, stretched himself, and wagged his tail. The dumb nobleman ran to tell the good news to the king, and all the counsellors came back in a long train from the bottom of the sea, and set about the affairs of state as if nothing had happened.

The old king welcomed his children with open arms, and they all lived happily to the end of their days.

# THE WIDOWS AND THE STRANGERS.

In days of yore, there were once two poor old widows who lived in the same hamlet and under the same roof. But though the cottages joined and one roof covered them, they had each a separate dwelling; and although they were alike in age and circumstances, yet in other respects they were very different. For one dame was covetous, though she had little to save, and the other was liberal, though she had little to give.

Now, on the rising ground opposite to the widows' cottages, stood a monastery where a few pious and charitable brethren spent their time in prayer, labour, and good works. And with the alms of these monks, and the kindness of neighbours, and because their wants were few, the old women dwelt in comfort, and had daily bread, and lay warm at night.

One evening, when the covetous old widow was having supper, there came a knock at her door. Before she opened it she hastily put away the remains of her meal.

"For," said she, "it is a stormy night, and ten to one some belated vagabond wants shelter; and when there are victuals on the table every fool must be asked to sup."

But when she opened the door, a monk came in who had his cowl pulled over his head to shelter him from the storm. The widow was much disconcerted at having kept one of the brotherhood waiting, and loudly apologized, but the monk stopped her, saying, "I fear I cut short your evening meal, my daughter."

"Now in the name of ill-luck, how came he to guess that?" thought the widow, as with anxious civility she pressed the monk to take some supper after his walk; for the good woman always felt hospitably inclined towards any one who was likely to return her kindness sevenfold.

The brother, however, refused to sup; and as he seated himself the widow looked sharply through her spectacles to see if she could gather from any distention of the folds of his frock whether a loaf, a bottle of cordial, or a new winter's cloak were most likely to crown the visit. No undue protuberance being visible about the monk's person, she turned her eyes to his face, and found that her visitor was one of the brotherhood whom she had not seen before. And not only was his face unfamiliar, it was utterly unlike the kindly but rough countenances of her charitable patrons. None that she had ever seen boasted the noble beauty, the chiselled and refined features of the monk before her. And she could not but notice that, although only one rushlight illumined her room, and though the monk's cowl went far to shade him even from that, yet his face was lit up as if by light from within, so that his clear skin seemed almost transparent. In short, her curiosity must have been greatly stirred, had not greed made her more anxious to learn what he had brought than who he was.

"It's a terrible night," quoth the monk, at length. "Such tempest without only gives point to the indoor comforts of the wealthy; but it chills the very marrow of the poor and destitute."

"Aye, indeed," sniffed the widow, with a shiver. "If it were not for the charity of good Christians, what would poor folk do for comfort on such an evening as this?"

"It was that very thought, my daughter," said the monk, with a sudden earnestness on his shining face, "that brought me forth even now through the storm to your cottage."

"Heaven reward you!" cried the widow, fervently.

"Heaven does reward the charitable!" replied the monk. "To no truth do the Scriptures bear such constant and unbroken witness; even as it is written: 'He that hath pity upon the poor lendeth unto the Lord; and look, what he layeth out it shall be paid him again.'"

"What a blessed thing it must be to be able to do good!" sighed the widow, piously wishing in her heart that the holy man would not delay to earn his recompense.

"My daughter," said the monk, "that blessing is not withheld from you. It is to ask your help for those in greater need than yourself that I am come to-night." And forthwith the good brother began to tell how two strangers had sought shelter at the monastery. Their house had been struck by lightning, and burnt with all it contained; and they themselves, aged, poor, and friendless, were exposed to the fury of the storm. "Our house is a poor one," continued the monk. "The strangers' lodging room was already full, and we are quite without the means of making these poor souls comfortable. You at least have a sound roof over your head, and if you can spare one or two things for the night, they shall be restored to you to-morrow, when some of our guests depart."

The widow could hardly conceal her vexation and disappointment. "Now, dear heart, holy father!" cried she, "is there not a rich body in the place, that you come for charity to a poor old widow like me, that am in a case rather to borrow myself than to lend to others?"

"Can you spare us a blanket?" said the monk. "These poor strangers have been out in the storm, remember."

The widow started. "What meddling busybody told him that the Baroness gave me a new blanket at Michaelmas?" thought she; but at last, very unwillingly, she went to an inner room to fetch a blanket from her bed.

"They shan't have the new one, that's flat," muttered the widow; and she drew out the old one and began to fold it up. But though she had made much of its thinness and insufficiency to the Baroness, she was so powerfully affected at parting with it, that all its good qualities came strongly to her mind.

"It's a very suitable size," she said to herself, "and easy for my poor old arms to shake or fold. With careful usage, it would last for years yet; but who knows how two wandering bodies that have been tramping miles through the storm may kick about in their sleep? And who knows if they're decent folk at all? likely enough they're two hedge birds, who have imposed a pitiful tale on the good fathers, and never slept under anything finer than a shock of straw in their lives."

The more the good woman thought of this, the more sure she felt that such was the case, and the less willing she became to lend her blanket to "a couple of good-for-nothing tramps." A sudden idea decided her. "Ten to one they bring fever with them!" she cried; "and dear knows I saw enough good bedding burnt after the black fever, three years ago! It would be a sin and a shame to burn a good blanket like this." And repeating "a sin and a shame" with great force, the widow restored the blanket to its place.

"The coverlet's not worth much," she thought; "but my goodman bought it the year after we were married, and if anything happened to it I should never forgive myself. The old shawl is good enough for tramps." Saying which she took a ragged old shawl from a peg, and began to fold it up. But even as she brushed and folded, she begrudged the faded rag.

"It saves my better one on a bad day," she sighed; "but I suppose the father must have something."

And accordingly she took it to the monk, saying, "It's not so good as it has been, but there's warmth in it yet, and it cost a pretty penny when new."

"And is this all that you can spare to the poor houseless strangers?" asked the monk.

"Aye, indeed, good father," said she, "and that will cost me many a twinge of rheumatics. Folk at my age can't lie cold at night for nothing."

"These poor strangers," said the monk, "are as aged as yourself, and have lost everything."

But as all he said had no effect in moving the widow's compassion, he departed, and knocked at the door of her neighbour. Here he told the same tale, which met with a very different hearing. This widow was one of those liberal souls whose possessions always make them feel uneasy unless they are being accepted, or used, or borrowed by some one else. She blessed herself that, thanks to the Baroness, she had a new blanket fit to lend to the king himself, and only desired to know with what else she could serve the poor strangers and requite the charities of the brotherhood.

The monk confessed that all the slender stock of household goods in the monastery was in use, and one after another he accepted the loan of almost everything the widow had. As she gave the things he put them out through the door, saying that he had a messenger outside; and having promised that all should be duly restored on the morrow, he departed, leaving the widow with little else than an old chair in which she was to pass the night.

When the monk had gone, the storm raged with greater fury than before, and at last one terrible flash of lightning struck the widows' house, and though it did not hurt the old women, it set fire to the roof, and both cottages were soon ablaze. Now as the terrified old creatures hobbled out into the storm, they met the monk, who, crying, "Come to the monastery!" seized an arm of each, and hurried them up the hill. To such good purpose did he help them, that they seemed to fly, and arrived at the convent gate they hardly knew how.

Under a shed by the wall were the goods and chattels of the liberal widow.

"Take back thine own, daughter," said the monk; "thy charity hath brought its own reward."

"But the strangers, good father?" said the perplexed widow.

"Ye are the strangers," answered the monk; "and what thy pity thought meet to be spared for the unfortunate, Heaven in thy misfortune hath spared to thee."

Then turning to the other widow, he drew the old shawl from beneath his frock, and gave it to her, saying, "I give you joy, dame, that this hath escaped the flames. It is not so good as it has been; but there is warmth in it yet, and it cost a pretty penny when new."

Full of confusion, the illiberal widow took back her shawl, murmuring, "Lack-a-day! If I had but known it was ourselves the good father meant!"

The monk gave a shrewd smile.

"Aye, aye, it would have been different, I doubt not," said he; "but accept the lesson, my daughter, and when next thou art called upon to help the unfortunate, think that it is thine own needs that would be served; and it may be thou shalt judge better as to what thou canst spare."

As he spoke, a flash of lightning lit up the ground where the monk stood, making a vast aureole about him in the darkness of the night. In the bright light, his countenance appeared stern and awful in its beauty, and when the flash was passed, the monk had vanished also.

Furthermore, when the widows sought shelter in the monastery, they found that the brotherhood knew nothing of their strange visitor.

# KIND WILLIAM AND THE WATER SPRITE.

There once lived a poor weaver, whose wife died a few years after their marriage. He was now alone in the world except for their child, who was a very quick and industrious little lad, and, moreover, of such an obliging disposition that he gained the nickname of Kind William.

On his seventh birthday his father gave him a little net with a long handle, and with this Kind William betook himself to a shallow part of the river to fish. After wandering on for some time, he found a quiet pool dammed in by stones, and here he dipped for the minnows that darted about in the clear brown water. At the first and second casts he caught nothing, but with the third he landed no less than twenty-one little fishes, and such minnows he had never seen, for as they leaped and struggled in the net they shone with alternate tints of green and gold.

He was gazing at them with wonder and delight, when a voice behind him cried, in piteous tones—

"Oh, my little sisters! Oh, my little sisters!"

Kind William turned round, and saw, sitting on a rock that stood out of the stream, a young girl weeping bitterly. She had a very pretty face, and abundant yellow hair of marvellous length, and of such uncommon brightness that even in the shade it shone like gold. She was dressed in grass green, and from her knees downwards she was hidden by the clumps of fern and rushes that grew by the stream.

"What ails you, my little lass?" said Kind William.

But the maid only wept more bitterly, and wringing her hands, repeated, "Oh, my little sisters! Oh, my little sisters!" presently adding in the same tone, "The little fishes! Oh, the little fishes!"

"Dry your eyes, and I will give you half of them," said the good-natured child; "and if you have no net you shall fish with me this afternoon."

But at this proposal the maid's sobs redoubled, and she prayed and begged with frantic eagerness that he would throw the fish back into the river. For some time Kind William would not consent to throw away his prize, but at last he yielded to her excessive grief, and emptied the net into the pool, where the glittering fishes were soon lost to sight under the sand and pebbles.

The girl now laughed and clapped her hands.

"This good deed you shall never rue, Kind William," said she, "and even now it shall repay you threefold. How many fish did you catch?"

"Twenty-one," said Kind William, not without regret in his tone.

The maid at once began to pull hairs out of her head, and did not stop till she had counted sixty-three, and laid them together in her fingers. She then began to wind the lock up into a curl, and it took far longer to wind than the sixty-three hairs had taken to pull. How long her hair really was Kind William never could tell, for after it reached her knees he lost sight of it among the fern; but he began to suspect that she was no true village maid, but a water sprite, and he heartily wished himself safe at home.

"Now," said she, when the lock was wound, "will you promise me three things?"

"If I can do so without sin," said Kind William.

"First," she continued, holding out the lock of hair, "will you keep this carefully, and never give it away? It will be for your own good."

"One never gives away gifts," said Kind William, "I promise that."

"The second thing is to spare what you have spared. Fish up the river and down the river at your will, but swear never to cast net in this pool again."

"One should not do kindness by halves," said Kind William. "I promise that also."

"Thirdly, you must never tell what you have now seen and heard till thrice seven years have passed. And now come hither, my child, and give me your little finger, that I may see if you can keep a secret."

But by this time Kind William's hairs were standing on end, and he gave the last promise more from fear than from any other motive, and seized his net to go.

"No hurry, no hurry," said the maiden (and the words sounded like the rippling of a brook over pebbles). Then bending towards him, with a strange smile, she added, "You are afraid that I shall pinch too hard, my pretty boy. Well, give me a farewell kiss before you go."

"I kiss none but the miller's lass," said Kind William, sturdily; for she was his little sweetheart. Besides, he was afraid that the water witch would enchant him and draw him down. At his answer she laughed till the echoes rang, but Kind William shuddered to hear that the echoes seemed to come from the river instead of from the hills; and they rang in his ears like a distant torrent leaping over rocks.

"Then listen to my song," said the water sprite. With which she drew some of her golden hairs over her arm, and tuning them as if they had been the strings of a harp, she began to sing:

"Warp of woollen and woof of gold: When seven and seven and seven are told."

But when Kind William heard that the river was running with the cadence of the tune, he could bear it no longer, and took to his heels. When he had run a few yards he heard a splash, as if a salmon had jumped, and on looking back he found that the yellow-haired maiden was gone.

Kind William was trustworthy as well as obliging, and he kept his word. He said nothing of his adventure. He put the yellow lock into an old china teapot that had stood untouched on the mantelpiece for years. And fishing up the river and down the river he never again cast net into the haunted pool. And in course of time the whole affair passed from his mind.

Fourteen years went by, and Kind William was Kind William still. He was as obliging as ever, and still loved the miller's daughter, who, for her part, had not forgotten her old playmate. But the miller's memory was not so good, for the fourteen years had been prosperous ones with him, and he was rich, whereas they had only brought bad trade and poverty to the weaver and his son. So the lovers were not allowed even to speak to each other.

One evening Kind William wandered by the river-side lamenting his hard fate. It was his twenty-first birthday, and he might not even receive the good wishes of the day from his old playmate. It was just growing dusk, a time when prudent bodies hurry home from the neighbourhood of fairy rings, sprite-haunted streams, and the like, and Kind William was beginning to quicken his pace, when a voice from behind him sang:

"Warp of woollen and woof of gold: When seven and seven and seven are told."

Kind William felt sure that he had heard this before, though he could not recall when or where; but suspecting that it was no mortal voice that sang, he hurried home without looking behind him. Before he reached the house he remembered all, and also that on this very day his promise of secrecy expired.

Meanwhile the old weaver had been sadly preparing the loom to weave a small stock of yarn, which he had received in payment for some work. He had set up the warp, and was about to fill the shuttle, when his son came in and told the story, and repeated the water sprite's song.

"Where is the lock of hair, my son?" asked the old man.

"In the teapot still, if you have not touched it," said Kind William; "but the dust of fourteen years must have destroyed all gloss and colour."

On searching the teapot, however, the lock of hair was found to be as bright as ever, and it lay in the weaver's hand like a coil of gold.

"It is the song that puzzles me," said Kind William. "Seven, and seven, and seven make twenty-one. Now that is just my age."

"There is your warp of woollen, if that is anything," added the weaver, gazing at the loom with a melancholy air.

"And this is golden enough," laughed Kind William, pointing to the curl. "Come, father, let us see how far one hair will go on the shuttle." And suiting the action to the word, he began to wind. He wound the shuttle full, and then sat down to the loom and began to throw.

The result was a fabric of such beauty that the Weavers shouted with amazement, and one single hair served for the woof of the whole piece.

Before long there was not a town dame or a fine country lady but must needs have a dress of the new stuff, and before the sixty-three hairs were used up, the fortunes of the weaver and his son were made.

About this time the miller's memory became clearer, and he was often heard to speak of an old boy-and-girl love between his dear daughter and the wealthy manufacturer of the golden cloth. Within a year and a day Kind William married his sweetheart, and as money sticks to money, in the end he added the old miller's riches to his own.

Moreover there is every reason to believe that he and his wife lived happily to the end of their days.

And what became of the water sprite?

That you must ask somebody else, for I do not know.

## MURDOCH'S RATH.[8]

There was not a nicer boy in all Ireland than Pat, and clever at his trade too, if only he'd had one.

But from his cradle he learned nothing (small blame to him with no one to teach him!), so when he came to years of discretion, he earned his living by running messages for his neighbours; and Pat could always be trusted to make the best of a bad bargain, and bring back all the change, for he was the soul of honesty and good-nature.

It's no wonder then that he was beloved by every one, and got as much work as he could do, and if the pay had but fitted the work, he'd have been mighty comfortable; but as it was, what he got wouldn't have kept him in shoe-leather, but for making both ends meet by wearing his shoes in his pocket, except when he was in the town, and obliged to look genteel for the credit of the place he came from.

Well, all was going on as peaceable as could be, till one market-day, when business (or it may have been pleasure) detained him till the heel of the evening, and by nightfall, when he began to make the road short in good earnest, he was so flustered, rehearsing his messages to make sure he'd forgotten nothing, that he never bethought him to leave off his brogues, but tramped on just as if shoe-leather were made to be knocked to bits on the king's highway.

And this was what he was after saying:

"A dozen hanks of grey yarn for Mistress Murphy."

"Three gross of bright buttons for the tailor."

"Half an ounce of throat drops for Father Andrew, and an ounce of snuff for his housekeeper," and so on.

For these were what he went to the town to fetch, and he was afraid lest one of the lot might have slipped his memory.

Now everybody knows there are two ways home from the town; and that's not meaning the right way and the wrong way, which my grandmother (rest her soul!) said there was to every place but one that it's not genteel to name. (There could only be a wrong way there, she said.) The two ways home from the town were the highway, and the way by Murdoch's Rath.

Murdoch's Rath was a pleasant enough spot in the daytime, but not many persons cared to go by it when the sun was down. And in all the years Pat was going backwards and forwards, he never once came home except by the high-road till this unlucky evening, when, just at the place where the two roads part, he got, as one may say, into a sort of confusion.

"Halt!" says he to himself (for his own uncle had been a soldier, and Pat knew the word of command). "The left-hand turn is the right one," says he, and he was going down the high-road as straight as he could go, when suddenly he bethought himself. "And what am I doing?" he says. "This was my left hand going to town, and how in the name of fortune could it be my left going back, considering that I've turned round? It's well that I looked into it in time." And with that he went off as fast down the other road as he started down this.

But how far he walked he never could tell, before all of a sudden the moon shone out as bright as day, and Pat found himself in Murdoch's Rath.

And this was the smallest part of the wonder; for the Rath was full of fairies.

When Pat got in they were dancing round and round till his feet tingled to look at them, being a good dancer himself. And as he sat on the side of the Rath, and snapped his fingers to mark the time, the dancing stopped, and a little man comes up, in a black hat and a green coat, with white stockings, and red shoes on his feet.

"Won't you take a turn with us, Pat?" says he, bowing till he nearly touched the ground. And, indeed, he had not far to go, for he was barely two feet high.

"Don't say it twice, sir," says Pat. "It's myself will be proud to foot the floor wid ye;" and before you could look round, there was Pat in the circle dancing away for bare life.

At first his feet felt like feathers for lightness, and it seemed as if he could have gone on for ever. But at last he grew tired, and would have liked to stop, but the fairies would not, and so they danced on and on. Pat tried to think of something good to say, that he might free himself from the spell, but all he could think of was:

"A dozen hanks of grey yarn for Missis Murphy."

"Three gross of bright buttons for the tailor."

"Half an ounce of throat drops for Father Andrew, and an ounce of snuff for his housekeeper," and so on.

And it seemed to Pat that the moon was on the one side of the Rath when they began to dance, and on the other side when they left off; but he could not be sure after all that going round. One thing was plain enough. He danced every bit of leather off the soles of his feet, and they were blistered so that he could hardly stand; but all the little folk did was to stand and hold their sides with laughing at him.

At last the one who spoke before stepped up to him, and—"Don't break your heart about it, Pat," says he; "I'll lend you my own shoes till the morning, for you seem to be a good-natured sort of a boy."

Well, Pat looked at the fairy man's shoes, that were the size of a baby's, and he looked at his own feet; but not wishing to be uncivil, "Thank ye kindly, sir," says he. "And if your honour 'll be good enough to put them on for me, maybe you won't spoil the shape." For he thought to himself, "Small blame to me if the little gentleman can't get them to fit."

With that he sat down on the side of the Rath, and the fairy man put on the shoes for him, and no sooner did they touch Pat's feet, than they became altogether a convenient size, and fitted him like wax. And, more than that, when he stood up, he didn't feel his blisters at all.

"Bring 'em back to the Rath at sunrise, Pat, my boy," says the little man.

And as Pat was climbing over the ditch, "Look round, Pat," says he. And when Pat looked round, there were jewels and pearls lying at the roots of the furze-bushes on the ditch, as thick as peas.

"Will you help yourself, or take what's given ye, Pat?" says the fairy man.

"Did I ever learn manners?" says Pat. "Would you have me help myself before company? I'll take what your honour pleases to give me, and be thankful."

The fairy man picked a lot of yellow furze-blossoms from the bushes, and filled Pat's pockets. "Keep 'em for love, Pat, me darlin'," says he.

Pat would have liked some of the jewels, but he put the furze-blossoms by for love.

"Good-evening to your honour," says he.

"And where are you going, Pat, dear?" says the fairy man.

"I'm going home," says Pat. And if the fairy man didn't know where that was, small blame to him.

"Just let me dust them shoes for ye, Pat," says the fairy man. And as Pat lifted up each foot he breathed on it, and dusted it with the tail of his green coat.

"Home!" says he, and when he let go, Pat was at his own doorstep before he could look round, and his parcels safe and sound with him.

Next morning he was up with the sun, and carried the fairy man's shoes back to the Rath. As he came up, the little man looked over the ditch.

"The top of the morning to, your honour," says Pat; "here's your shoes."

"You're an honest boy, Pat," says the little gentleman. "It's inconvenienced I am without them, for. I have but the one pair. Have you looked at the yellow flowers this morning?" he says.

"I have not, sir," says Pat; "I'd be loth to deceive you. I came off as soon as I was up."

"Be sure to look when you get back, Pat," says the fairy man, "and good luck to ye."

With which he disappeared, and Pat went home. He looked for the furze-blossoms, as the fairy man told him, and there's not a word of truth in this tale if they weren't all pure gold pieces.

Well, now Pat was so rich, he went to the shoemaker to order another pair of brogues, and being a kindly, gossiping boy, the shoemaker soon learned the whole story of the fairy man and the Rath. And this so stirred up the shoemaker's greed that he resolved to go the very next night himself, to see if he could not dance with the fairies, and have like luck.

He found his way to the Rath all correct, and sure enough the fairies were dancing, and they asked him to join. He danced the soles off his brogues, as Pat did, and the fairy man lent him his shoes, and sent him home in a twinkling.

As he was going over the ditch, he looked round, and saw the roots of the furze-bushes glowing with precious stones as if they had been glow-worms.

"Will you help yourself, or take what's given ye?" said the fairy man.

"I'll help myself, if you please," said the cobbler, for he thought—"If I can't get more than Pat brought home, my fingers must all be thumbs."

So he drove his hand into the bushes, and if he didn't get plenty, it wasn't for want of grasping.

When he got up in the morning, he went straight to the jewels. But not a stone of the lot was more precious than roadside pebbles. "I ought not to look till I come from the Rath," said he. "It's best to do like Pat all through."

But he made up his mind not to return the fairy man's shoes.

"Who knows the virtue that's in them?" he said. So he made a small pair of red leather shoes, as like them as could be, and he blacked the others upon his feet, that the fairies might not know them, and at sunrise he went to the Rath.

The fairy man was looking over the ditch as before.

"Good-morning to you," said he.

"The top of the morning to you, sir," said the cobbler; "here's your shoes." And he handed him the pair that he had made, with a face as grave as a judge.

The fairy man looked at them, but he said nothing, though he did not put them on.

"Have you looked at the things you got last night?" says he.

"I'll not deceive you, sir," says the cobbler. "I came off as soon as I was up. Sorra peep I took at them."

"Be sure to look when you get back," says the fairy man. And just as the cobbler was getting over the ditch to go home, he says:

"If my eyes don't deceive me," says he, "there's the least taste in life of dirt on your left shoe. Let me dust it with the tail of my coat."

"That means home in a twinkling," thought the cobbler, and he held up his foot.

The fairy man dusted it, and muttered something the cobbler did not hear. Then, "Sure," says he, "it's the dirty pastures that you've come through, for the other shoe's as bad."

So the cobbler held up his right foot, and the fairy man rubbed that with the tail of his green coat.

When all was done the cobbler's feet seemed to tingle, and then to itch, and then to smart, and then to burn. And at last he began to dance, and he danced all round the Rath (the fairy man laughing and holding his sides), and then round and round again. And he danced till he cried out with weariness, and tried to shake the shoes off. But they stuck fast, and the fairies drove him over, the ditch, and through the prickly furze-bushes, and he danced away. Where he danced to, I cannot tell you. Whether he ever got rid of the fairy shoes, I do not know. The jewels never were more than wayside pebbles, and they were swept out when his cabin was cleaned, which was not too soon, you may be sure.

All this happened long ago; but there are those who say that the covetous cobbler dances still, between sunset and sunrise, round Murdoch's Rath.

# THE LITTLE DARNER.

In days gone by there lived a poor widow who had brought up her only child so well that the little lass was more helpful and handy than many a grown-up person.

When other women's children were tearing and dirtying their clothes, clamouring at their mothers' skirts for this and that, losing and breaking and spoiling things, and getting into mischief of all kinds, the widow's little girl, with her tiny thimble on her finger, could patch quite neatly. She was to be trusted to put anything in its proper place, and when meals were over she would stand on a little stool at the table washing up the dishes. Moreover, she could darn stockings so well that the darn looked like a part of the stocking. The slatternly mothers, who spoiled and scolded their children by turns, and had never taught them to be tidy and obedient, used often to quote the widow's little girl to their troublesome brats, and say, "Why don't you help your mother as the widow's daughter helps her?"

Thus it came about that the helpless, useless, untidy little girls hated the very name of the widow's daughter, because they were always being told of her usefulness and neatness.

Now the widow's child often earned a few pence by herding sheep or pigs for the farmers, or by darning stockings for their wives, and as she could be trusted, people were very glad to employ her. One day she was keeping watch over five little pigs in a field, and, not to waste time, was darning a pair of stockings as well, when some of the little girls who had a spite against her resolved to play her a trick.

Near the field where the little maid and the pigs were there was a wood, into which all children were strictly forbidden to go. For in the depths of the wood there lived a terrible Ogre and Ogress, who kidnapped all children who strayed near their dwelling. Every morning the Ogre threw a big black bag over his shoulder, and stalked through the forest, making the ground shake as he walked. If he found any truant children he popped them into his bag, and when he got home his wife cooked them for supper.

The trick played upon the widow's daughter was this. Five little girls came up to the field where she was herding the five little pigs, and each chasing a pig, they drove them into the Ogre's wood. In vain the little maid called to her flock; the pigs ran in a frightened troop into the wood, and she ran after them. When the five little girls saw that she had got them together again, they ran in to chase them away once more, and so they were all in the wood together, when the ground shook under them, upsetting the six little girls and the five little pigs; and as they rolled over the Ogre picked them up, and put them one after another into his bag.

When they were jolting about with the pigs in the poke as the Ogre strode homewards, the five spiteful children were as sorry as you please; and as the pigs were always fighting and struggling to get to the top, they did not escape without some scratches. And their screams, and the squealing of the little pigs made such a noise that the Ogre's wife heard it a mile and a half away in the depths of the wood; and she lighted a fire under the copper, and filled it with water, ready to cook whatever her husband brought home.

As for the widow's little daughter she pulled her needle-book from her pocket, and every now and then she pushed a needle through the sack, that it might fall on the ground, and serve as a guide if she should ever have the chance of finding her way home again.

When the Ogre arrived, he emptied the sack, and sent the six little girls and the five little pigs all sprawling on to the floor, saying:

"These will last us some time. Cook the fattest, and put the rest into the cellar. And whilst you get dinner ready, I will take another stroll with the bag. Luck seldom comes singly."

When he had gone, the Ogress looked over the children, and picked out the widow's daughter, saying:

"You look the most good-humoured. And the best-tempered always make the best eating."

So she set her down on a stool by the fire till the water should boil, and locked the others up in the cellar.

"Tears won't put the fire out," thought the little maid. So instead of crying she pulled out the old stocking, and went on with her darning. When the Ogress came back from the cellar she went up to her and looked at her work.

"How you darn!" she cried. "Now that's a sort of thing I hate. And the Ogre does wear such big holes in his stockings, and his feet are so large, that, though my hand is not a small one, I cannot fill out the heel with my fist, and then who's to darn it neatly I should like to know?"

"If I had a basin big enough to fill out the heel, I think I could do it," said the little maid.

The Ogress scratched her big ear thoughtfully for a minute, and then she said:

"To lose a chance is to cheat oneself. Why shouldn't this one darn while the others boil? Yes, I think you shall try. Six days ought to serve for mending all the stockings, though the Ogre hasn't a whole pair left, and angry enough he'll be. And when household matters are not to his mind he puts that big sack over my head, and ties it round my neck. And if you had ever done housework with your head in a poke, you'd know what it is! So you shall darn the stockings, and if you do them well, I'll cook one of the others first instead of you."

Saying which, the Ogress fetched one of the Ogre's stockings, and the widow's child put a big basin into the heel to stretch it, and began to darn. The Ogress watched her till she had put all the threads one way, and when she began to run the cross threads, interlacing them with the utmost exactness, the old creature was delighted, and went to fetch another child to be cooked instead of the widow's.

When the other little girl came up, she cried and screamed so that the room rang with her lamentations, and the widow's child laid down her needle and ceased working.

"Why don't you go on darning?" asked the Ogress.

"Alas! dear mother," said she, "the little sister's cries make my heart beat so that I cannot darn evenly."

"Then she must go back to the cellar for a bit," said the Ogress. "And meanwhile I'll sharpen the knife."

So after she had taken back the crying child, and had watched the little girl, who now darned away as skilfully as ever, the Ogress took down a huge knife from the wall, and began to sharpen it on a grindstone in a corner of the kitchen. As she sharpened the knife, she glanced from time to time at the little maid, and soon perceived that she had once more ceased working.

"Why don't you go on darning?" asked the Ogress.

"Alas! dear mother," said the child, "when I hear you sharpening that terrible knife my hands tremble so that I cannot thread my needle."

"Well, it will do now," growled the Ogress, feeling the edge of the blade with her horny finger; and, having seen the darning-needle once more at work, she went to fetch up one of the children. As she went, she hummed what cookmaids sing—

"Dilly, dilly duckling, come and be killed!"

But it sounded like the wheezing and groaning of a heavy old door upon its rusty hinges.

When she came in, with the child in one hand, and the huge knife in the other, she went up to the little darner to look at her work. The heel of the Ogre's stocking was exquisitely mended, all but seven threads; but the little maid sat idle with her hands before her.

"Why don't you go on darning?" asked the Ogress.

"Alas! dear mother," was the reply, "when I think of my little playmate about to die, the tears blind my eyes, so that I cannot see what stitches I take. Wherefore I beg of you, dear mother, to cook one of the little pigs instead, that I may be able to go on with my work, and that a pair of stockings may be ready to-morrow morning when the Ogre will ask for them; so my playmate's life will be spared, and your head will not be put into a poke."

At first the Ogress would not hear of such a thing, but at last she consented, and made a stew of one of the little pigs instead of cooking the little girl.

"But supposing the Ogre goes to count the children," said she; "he will find one too many."

"Then let her go, dear mother," said the widow's daughter; "she will find her way home, and you will never be blamed."

"But she must stir the stew with her forefinger first," said the Ogress, "that it may have a human flavour."

So the little girl had to stir the hot stew with her finger, which scalded it badly; and then she was set at liberty, and ran home as hard as she could; and as the little maid's needles sparkled here and there on the path, she had no difficulty in finding her way.

The Ogre was quite contented with his dinner, and the Ogress got great praise for the way in which she had darned his stockings. Thus it went on for four days more. As the widow's little girl wouldn't work if her companions were killed, the Ogress cooked the pigs one after another, and the children were all sent away with burnt forefingers.

When the fifth had been dismissed, and all the pigs were eaten, the Ogress said:

"To-morrow you will have to be stewed, and now I wish I had kept one of the others that I might have saved you altogether to work for me. However, there is one comfort, the stockings are finished."

But meanwhile the other children had got safely home, and had told their tale. And all the men of the place set off at once to attack the Ogre, and release the widow's child. Guided by the needles, they arrived just as the Ogress was sharpening the big knife for the last time.

So they killed the Ogre and his wife, and took the industrious little maid back to her mother.

The other little girls were now very repentant; and when their fingers were well, they all learned to darn stockings at once.

And as there was now no danger about going into the wood, it was no longer forbidden. And this being the case, the children were much less anxious to play there than formerly.

## THE FIDDLER IN THE FAIRY RING.

Generations ago, there once lived a farmer's son, who had no great harm in him, and no great good either. He always meant well, but he had a poor spirit, and was too fond of idle company.

One day his father sent him to market with some sheep for sale, and when business was over for the day, the rest of the country-folk made ready to go home, and more than one of them offered the lad a lift in his cart.

"Thank you kindly, all the same," said he, "but I am going back across the downs with Limping Tim."

Then out spoke a steady old farmer and bade the lad go home with the rest, and by the main road. For Limping Tim was an idle, graceless kind of fellow, who fiddled for his livelihood, but what else he did to earn the money he squandered, no one knew. And as to the sheep path over the downs, it stands to reason that the highway is better travelling after sunset, for the other is no such very short cut; and has a big fairy ring so near it, that a butter-woman might brush it with the edge of her market cloak, as she turned the brow of the hill.

But the farmer's son would go his own way, and that was with Limping Tim, and across the downs.

So they started, and the fiddler had his fiddle in his hand, and a bundle of marketings under his arm, and he sang snatches of strange songs, the like of which the lad had never heard before. And the moon drew out their shadows over the short grass till they were as long as the great stones of Stonehenge.

At last they turned the hill, and the fairy ring looked dark under the moon, and the farmer's son blessed himself that they were passing it quietly, when Limping Tim suddenly pulled his cloak from his back, and handing it to his companion, cried, "Hold this for a moment, will you? I'm wanted. They're calling for me."

"I hear nothing," said the farmer's son. But before he had got the words out of his mouth, the fiddler had completely disappeared. He shouted aloud, but in vain, and had begun to think of proceeding on his way, when the fiddler's voice cried, "Catch!" and there came, flying at him from the direction of the fairy ring, the bundle of marketings which the fiddler had been carrying.

"It's in my way," he then heard the fiddler cry. "Ah, this is dancing! Come in, my lad, come in!"

But the farmer's son was not totally without prudence, and he took good care to keep at a safe distance from the fairy ring.

"Come back, Tim! Come back!" he shouted, and, receiving no answer, he adjured his friend to break the bonds that withheld him, and return to the right way, as wisely as one man can counsel another.

After talking for some time to no purpose, he again heard his friend's voice, crying, "Take care of it for me! The money dances out of my pocket." And therewith the fiddler's purse was hurled to his feet, where it fell with a heavy chinking of gold within.

He picked it up, and renewed his warnings and entreaties, but in vain; and, after waiting for a long time, he made the best of his way home alone, hoping that the fiddler would follow, and come to reclaim his property.

The fiddler never came. And when at last there was a fuss about his disappearance, the farmer's son, who had but a poor spirit, began to be afraid to tell the truth of the matter. "Who knows but they may accuse me of theft?" said he. So he hid the cloak, and the bundle, and the money-bag in the garden.

But when three months passed, and still the fiddler did not return, it was whispered that the farmer's son had been his last companion; and the place was searched, and they found the cloak, and the bundle, and the money-bag and the lad was taken to prison.

Now, when it was too late, he plucked up a spirit, and told the truth; but no one believed him, and it was said that he had murdered the fiddler for the sake of his money and goods. And he was taken before the judge, found guilty, and sentenced to death.

Fortunately, his old mother was a Wise Woman. And when she heard that he was condemned, she said, "Only follow my directions, and we may save you yet; for I guess how it is."

So she went to the judge, and begged for her son three favours before his death.

"I will grant them," said the judge, "if you do not ask for his life."

"The first," said the old woman, "is, that he may choose the place where the gallows shall be erected; the second, that he may fix the hour of his execution; and the third favour is, that you will not fail to be present."

"I grant all three," said the judge. But when he learned that the criminal had chosen a certain hill on the downs for the place of execution, and an hour before midnight for the time, he sent to beg the sheriff to bear him company on this important occasion.

The sheriff placed himself at the judge's disposal, but he commanded the attendance of the gaoler as some sort of protection; and the gaoler, for his part, implored his reverence the chaplain to be of the party, as the hill was not in good spiritual repute. So, when the time came, the four started together, and the hangman and the farmer's son went before them to the foot of the gallows.

Just as the rope was being prepared, the farmer'a son called to the judge, and said, "If your Honour will walk twenty paces down the hill, to where you will see a bit of paper, you will learn the fate of the fiddler."

"That is, no doubt, a copy of the poor man's last confession," thought the judge.

"Murder will out, Mr. Sheriff," said he; and in the interests of truth and justice he hastened to pick up the paper.

But the farmer's son had dropped it as he came along, by his mother's direction, in such a place that the judge could not pick it up without putting his foot on the edge of the fairy ring. No sooner had he done so than he perceived an innumerable company of little people dressed in green cloaks and hoods, who were dancing round in a circle as wide as the ring itself.

They were all about two feet high, and had aged faces, brown and withered, like the knots on gnarled trees in hedge bottoms, and they squinted horribly; but, in spite of their seeming age, they flew round and round like children.

"Mr. Sheriff! Mr. Sheriff!" cried the judge, "come and see the dancing. And hear the music, too, which is so lively that it makes the soles of my feet tickle."

"There is no music, my Lord Judge," said the sheriff, running down the hill. "It is the wind whistling over the grass that your lordship hears."

But when the sheriff had put his foot by the judge's foot, he saw and heard the same, and he cried out, "Quick, Gaoler, and come down! I should like you to be witness to this matter. And you may take my arm, Gaoler, for the music makes me feel unsteady."

"There is no music, sir," said the gaoler; "but your worship doubtless hears the creaking of the gallows."

But no sooner had the gaoler's feet touched the fairy ring, than he saw and heard like the rest, and he called lustily to the chaplain to come and stop the unhallowed measure.

"It is a delusion of the Evil One," said the parson; "there is not a sound in the air but the distant croaking of some frogs." But when he too touched the ring, he perceived his mistake.

At this moment the moon shone out, and in the middle of the ring they saw Limping Tim the fiddler, playing till great drops stood out on his forehead, and dancing as madly as he played.

"Ah, you rascal!" cried the judge. "Is this where you've been all the time, and a better man than you as good as hanged for you? But you shall come home now."

Saying which, he ran in, and seized the fiddler by the arm, but Limping Tim resisted so stoutly that the sheriff had to go to the judge's assistance, and even then the fairies so pinched and hindered them that the sheriff was obliged to call upon the gaoler to put his arms about his waist, who persuaded the chaplain to add his strength to the string. But as ill luck would have it, just as they were getting off, one of the fairies picked up Limping Tim's fiddle, which had fallen in the scuffle, and began to play. And as he began to play, every one began to dance—the fiddler, and the judge, and the sheriff, and the gaoler, and even the chaplain.

"Hangman! hangman!" screamed the judge, as he lifted first one leg and then the other to the tune, "come down, and catch hold of his reverence the chaplain. The prisoner is pardoned, and he can lay hold too."

The hangman knew the judge's voice, and ran towards it; but as they were now quite within the ring he could see nothing, either of him or his companions.

The farmer's son followed, and warning the hangman not to touch the ring, he directed him to stretch his hands forwards in hopes of catching hold of some one. In a few minutes the wind blew the chaplain's cassock against the hangman's fingers, and he caught the parson round the waist. The farmer's son then seized him in like fashion, and each holding firmly by the other, the fiddler, the judge, the sheriff, the gaoler, the parson, the hangman, and the farmer's son all got safely out of the charmed circle.

"Oh, you scoundrel!" cried the judge to the fiddler; "I have a very good mind to hang you up on the gallows without further ado."

But the fiddler only looked like one possessed, and upbraided the farmer's son for not having the patience to wait three minutes for him.

"Three minutes!" cried he; "why, you've been here three months and a day."

This the fiddler would not believe, and as he seemed in every way beside himself, they led him home, still upbraiding his companion, and crying continually for his fiddle.

His neighbours watched him closely, but one day he escaped from their care and wandered away over the hills to seek his fiddle, and came back no more.

His dead body was found upon the downs, face downwards, with the fiddle in his arms. Some said he had really found the fiddle where he had left it, and had been lost in a mist, and died of exposure. But others held that he had perished differently, and laid his death at the door of the fairy dancers.

As to the farmer's son, it is said that thenceforward he went home from market by the high-road, and spoke the truth straight out, and was more careful of his company.

## "I WON'T."

"Don't Care"—so they say—fell into a goose-pond; and "I won't" is apt to come to no better an end. At least, my grandmother tells me that was how the Miller had to quit his native town, and leave the tip of his nose behind him.

It all came of his being allowed to say "I won't" when he was quite a little boy. His mother thought he looked pretty when he was pouting, and that wilfulness gave him an air which distinguished him from other people's children. And when she found out that his lower lip was becoming so big that it spoilt his beauty, and that his wilfulness gained his way twice and stood in his way eight times out of ten, it was too late to alter him.

Then she said, "Dearest Abinadab, do be more obliging!"

And he replied (as she had taught him), "I won't."

He always took what he could get, and would neither give nor give up to other people. This, he thought, was the way to get more out of life than one's neighbours.

Amongst other things, he made a point of taking the middle of the footpath.

"Will you allow me to pass you, sir?—I am in a hurry," said a voice behind him one day.

"I won't," said Abinadab; on which a poor washerwoman, with her basket, scrambled down into the road, and Abinadab chuckled.

Next day he was walking as before.

"Will you allow me to pass you, sir?—I am in a hurry," said a voice behind him.

"I won't," said Abinadab. On which he was knocked into the ditch; and the Baron walked on, and left him to get out of the mud on whichever side he liked.

He quarrelled with his friends till he had none left, and he quarrelled with the tradesmen of the town till there was only one who would serve him, and this man offended him at last.

"I'll show you who's master!" said the Miller. "I won't pay a penny of your bill—not a penny."

"Sir," said the tradesman, "my giving you offence now, is no just reason why you should refuse to pay for what you have had and been satisfied with. I must beg you to pay me at once."

"I won't," said the Miller, "and what I say I mean. I won't; I tell you, I won't."

So the tradesman summoned him before the Justice, and the Justice condemned him to pay the bill and the costs of the suit.

"I won't," said the Miller.

So they put him in prison, and in prison he would have remained if his mother had not paid the money to obtain his release. By and by she died, and left him her blessing and some very good advice, which (as is sometimes the case with bequests) would have been more useful if it had come earlier.

The Miller's mother had taken a great deal of trouble off his hands which now fell into them. She took in all the small bags of grist which the country-folk brought to be ground, and kept account of them, and spoke civilly to the customers, big and little. But these small matters irritated the Miller.

"I may be the slave of all the old women in the country-side," said he; "but I won't—they shall see that I won't."

So he put up a notice to say that he would only receive grist at a certain hour on certain days. Now, but a third of the old women could read the notice, and they did not attend to it. People came as before; but the Miller locked the door of the mill and sat in the counting-house and chuckled.

"My good friend," said his neighbours, "you can't do business in this way. If a man lives by trade, he must serve his customers. And a Miller must take in grist when it comes to the mill."

"Others may if they please," said the Miller; "but I won't. When I make a rule, I stick to it."

"Take advice, man, or you'll be ruined," said his friends.

"I won't," said the Miller.

In a few weeks all the country-folk turned their donkeys' heads towards the windmill on the heath. It was a little farther to go, but the Windmiller took custom when it came to him, gave honest measure, and added civil words gratis.

The other Miller was ruined.

"All you can do now is to leave the mill while you can pay the rent, and try another trade," said his friends.

"I won't," said the Miller. "Shall I be turned out of the house where I was born, because the country-folk are fools?"

However, he could not pay the rent, and the landlord found another tenant.

"You must quit," said he to the Miller.

"That I won't," said the Miller, "not for fifty new tenants."

So the landlord sent for the constables, and he was carried out, which is not a dignified way of changing one's residence. But then it is not easy to be obstinate and dignified at the same time.

His wrath against the landlord knew no bounds.

"Was there ever such a brute?" he cried. "Would any man of spirit hold his home at the whim of a landlord? I'll never rent another house as long as I live."

"But you must live somewhere," said his friends.

"I won't," said the Miller.

He was no longer a young man, and the new tenant pitied him.

"The poor old fellow is out of his senses," he said. And he let him sleep in one of his barns. One of the mill cats found out that there was a new warm bed in this barn, and she came and lived there too, and kept away the mice.

One night, however, Mrs. Pussy disturbed the Miller's rest. She was in and out of the window constantly, and meowed horribly into the bargain.

"It seems a man can't even sleep in peace," said the Miller. "If this happens again, you'll go into the mill-race to sing to the fishes."

The next night the cat was still on the alert, and the following morning the Miller tied a stone round her neck, and threw her into the water.

"Oh, spare the poor thing, there's a good soul," said a bystander.

"I won't," said the Miller. "I told her what would happen."

When his back was turned, however, the bystander got Pussy out, and took her home with him.

Now the cat was away, the mice could play; and they played hide-and-seek over the Miller's nightcap.

It came to such a pass that there was no rest to be had.

"I won't go to bed, I declare I won't," said the Miller. So he sat up all night in an arm-chair, and threw everything he could lay his hands on at the corners where he heard the mice scuffling, till the place was topsy-turvy.

Towards morning he lit a candle and dressed himself. He was in a terrible humour; and when he began to shave, his hand shook and he cut himself. The draughts made the flame of the candle unsteady too, and the shadow of the Miller's nose (which was a large one) fell in uncertain shapes upon his cheeks, and interfered with the progress of the razor. At first he thought he would wait till daylight. Then his temper got the better of him.

"I won't," he said, "I won't; why should I?"

So he began again. He held on by his nose to steady his cheeks, and he gave it such a spiteful pinch that the tears came into his eyes.

"Matters have come to a pretty pass, when a man's own nose is to stand in his light," said he.

By and by a gust of wind came through the window. Up flared the candle, and the shadow of the Miller's nose danced half over his face, and the razor gashed his chin.

Transported with fury, he struck at it before he could think what he was doing. The razor was very sharp, and the tip of the Miller's nose came off as clean as his whiskers.

When daylight came, and he saw himself in the glass, he resolved to leave the place.

"I won't stay here to be a laughing-stock," said he.

As he trudged out on to the highway, with his bundle on his back, the Baron met him and pitied him. He dismounted from his horse, and leading it up to the Miller, he said:

"Friend, you are elderly to be going far afoot. I will lend you my mare to take you to your destination. When you are there, knot the reins and throw them on her shoulder, saying, 'Home!' She will then return to me. But mark one thing,—she is not used to whip or spur. Humour her, and she will carry you well and safely."

The Miller mounted willingly enough, and set forward. At first the mare was a little restive. The Miller had no spurs on, but, in spite of the Baron's warning, he kicked her with his heels. On this, she danced till the Miller's hat and bundle flew right and left, and he was very near to following them.

"Ah, you vixen!" he cried. "You think I'll humour you as the Baron does. But I won't—no, you shall see that I won't!" And gripping his walking-stick firmly in his hand, he belaboured the Baron's mare as if she had been a donkey.

On which she sent the Miller clean over her head, and cantered back to the castle; and wherever it was that he went to, he had to walk.

He never returned to his native village, and everybody was glad to be rid of him. One must bear and forbear with his neighbours, if he hopes to be regretted when he departs.

But my grandmother says that long after the mill had fallen into ruin, the story was told as a warning to wilful children of the Miller who cut off his nose to spite his own face.

# THE MAGIC JAR.

There was once a young fellow whom fortune had blessed with a good mother, a clever head, and a strong body. But beyond this she had not much favoured him; and though able and willing to work, he had often little to do, and less to eat. But his mother had taught him to be contented with his own lot, and to feel for others. Moreover, from her he inherited a great love for flowers.

One day, when his pockets were emptiest, a fair was held in the neighbouring town, and he must needs go as well as the rest, though he had no money to spend. But he stuck a buttercup in his cap, for which he had nothing to pay, and strode along as merrily as the most.

Towards evening some of the merrymakers became riotous; and a party of them fell upon an old Jew who was keeping a stall of glass and china, and would smash his stock. Now as the Jew stood before his booth beseeching them to spare his property, up came the strong young man, with the flower still unwithered in his cap, and he took the old Jew's part and defended him. For from childhood his mother had taught him to feel for others.

So those who would have ill-treated the old Jew now moved off, and the young man stayed with him till he had packed up his wares.

Then the Jew turned towards him and said, "My son, he who delivers the oppressed, and has respect unto the aged, has need of no reward, for the blessing of Him that blesseth is about him. Nevertheless, that I may not seem ungrateful, choose, I pray thee, one of these china jars; and take it to thee for thine own. If thou shalt choose well, it may be of more use to thee than presently appears."

Thereupon the young man examined the jars, which were highly ornamented with many figures and devices; but he chose one that was comparatively plain; only it had a bunch of flowers painted on the front, round which was a pretty device in spots or circles of gold.

Then said the Jew, "My son, why have you chosen this jar, when there are others so much finer?"

The young man said, "Because the flowers please me, and I have a love for flowers."

Then said the Jew, "Happy is he whose tastes are simple! Moreover, herein is a rare wisdom, and thou hast gained that which is the most valuable of my possessions. This jar has properties which I will further explain to thee. It was given to me by a wise woman, subject to this condition, that I must expose it for sale from sunrise to sunset at the yearly fair. When I understood this I took counsel with myself how I should preserve it; and I bought other china jars of more apparent value, and I marked them all with the same price. For I said within myself, 'There is no man who does not desire to get as much as he can for his money, therefore, from its contrast with these others, my jar is safe.' And it was even so; for truly, many have desired to buy the jar because of the delicate beauty of the flowers, if I would have sold it for less than others which seemed more valuable."

"Many times it has been almost gone, but when I have shown the others at the same price, my customers have reviled me, saying, 'Dog of a Jew, dost thou ask as much for this as for these others Which are manifestly worth double?' and they have either departed, cursing me, and taking nothing; or they have bought one of the more richly decorated jars at the same price. For verily in most men the spirit of covetousness is stronger than the love of beauty, and they rather desire to get much for their money, than to obtain that which is suitable and convenient."

"But in thee, O young man! I have beheld a rare wisdom. To choose that which is good in thine eyes, and suitable to thy needs, rather than that which satisfieth the lust of over-reaching; and lo! what I have so long kept from thousands, has become thine!"

Then the young man wished to restore to the Jew the jar he valued so highly, and to choose another.

But the Jew refused, saying, "A gift cannot be recalled. Moreover, I will now explain to thee its uses. Within the jar lies a toad, whose spit is poison. But it will never spit at its master. Every evening thou must feed it with bread and milk, when it will fall asleep; and at sunrise in the morning it will awake and breathe heavily against the side of the jar, which will thus become warm. As it warms the flowers will blossom out, and become real, and full of perfume, and thou wilt be able to pluck them without diminishing their number. Moreover, these twelve round spots of gold will drop off, and become twelve gold pieces, which will be thine. And thus it will be every day. Only thou must thyself rise with the sun, and gather the flowers and the gold with thine own hands. Furthermore, when the jar cools, the flowers and gilding will be as before. Fare thee well."

And even as he spoke the Jew lifted the huge crate of china on to his back, and disappeared among the crowd.

All came about as the Jew had promised. As he had twelve gold pieces a day, the young man now wanted for nothing, besides which he had fresh flowers on his table all the year round.

Now it is well said, "Thy business is my business, and the business of all beside;" for every man's affairs are his neighbours' property. Thus it came about that all those who lived near the young man were perplexed that he had such beautiful flowers in all seasons; and esteemed it as an injury to themselves that he should have them and give no explanation as to whence they came.

At last it came to the ears of the king, and he also was disturbed. For he was curious, and fond of prying into small matters; a taste which ill becomes those of high position. But the king had no child to succeed him; and he was always suspecting those about him of plotting to obtain the crown, and thus he came to be for ever prying into the affairs of his subjects.

Now when he heard of the young man who had flowers on his table all the year round, he desired one of his officers to go and question him as to how he obtained them. But the young man contrived to evade his questions, and the matter was at rest for a while.

Then the king sent another messenger, with orders to press the young man more closely; and because the young man disdained to tell a lie, he said, "I get the flowers from yon china jar."

Then the messenger returned, and said to the king, "The young man says that he gets the flowers from a certain china jar which stands in his room."

Then said the king, "Bring the contents of the jar hither to me." And the messenger returned and brought the toad.

But when the king laid hold upon the toad, it spat in his face; and he was poisoned and died.

Then the toad sat upon the king's mouth, and would not be enticed away. And every one feared to touch it because it spat poison. And they called the wise men of the council; and they performed certain rites to charm away the toad, and yet it would not go.

But after three days, the master of the toad came to the palace, and without saying who he was, he desired to be permitted to try and get the toad from the corpse of the king.

And when he was taken into the king's chamber, he stood and beckoned to the toad, saying, "The person of the king and the bodies of the dead are sacred, wherefore come away."

And the toad crawled from the king's face and came to him, and did not spit at him; and he put it back into the jar.

Then said the wise men, "There is no one so fit to succeed to the kingdom as this man is; both for wisdom of speech and for the power of command."

And what they said pleased the people; and the young man was made king. And in due time he married an amiable and talented princess, and had children. And he ruled the kingdom well and wisely, and was beloved till his death.

Now when, after the lapse of many years, he died, there was great grief among the people, and his body was laid out in his own room, and the people were permitted to come and look upon his face for the last time.

And among the crowd there appeared an aged Jew. And he did not weep as did the others; but he came and stood by the bier, and gazed upon the face of the dead king in silence. And after a while he exclaimed, and said:

"Oh, wonderful spectacle! A man, and not covetous. A ruler, and not oppressive. Contented in poverty, and moderate in wealth. Elect of the people, and beloved to the end!"

And when he had said this, he again became silent, and stood as one astonished.

And no one knew when he came in, nor perceived when he departed.

But when they came to search for the china jar, it was gone, and could never afterwards be found.

## THE FIRST WIFE'S WEDDING-RING.

Many years ago, there lived a certain worthy man who was twice married. By his first wife he had a son, who soon after his mother's death resolved to become a soldier, and go to foreign lands. "When one has seen the world, one values home the more," said he; "and if I live I shall return."

So the father gave him a blessing, and his mother's wedding-ring, saying, "Keep this ring, and then, however long you stay away, and however changed you may become, by this token I shall know you to be my true son and heir."

In a short time the father married again, and by this marriage also he had one son.

Years passed by, and the elder brother did not return, and at last every one believed him to be dead. But in reality he was alive, and after a long time he turned his steps homewards. He was so much changed by age and travelling that only his mother would have known him again, but he had the ring tied safe and fast round his neck. One night, however, he was too far from shelter to get a bed, so he slept under a hedge, and when he woke in the morning the string was untied and the ring was gone. He spent a whole day in searching for it, but in vain; and at last he resolved to proceed and explain the matter to his father.

The old man was overjoyed to see him, and fully believed his tale, but with the second wife it was otherwise. She was greatly displeased to think that her child was not now to be the sole heir of his father's goods; and she so pestered and worked upon the old man by artful and malicious speeches, that he consented to send away the new-comer till he should have found the first wife's wedding-ring.

"Is the homestead I have taken such care of," she cried, "to go to the first vagrant who comes in with a brown face and a ragged coat, pretending that he is your son?"

So the soldier was sent about his business; but his father followed him to the gate, and slipped some money into his hand, saying, "God speed you back again with the ring!"

It was Sunday morning, and the bells were ringing for service as he turned sadly away.

"Ding, dong!" rang the bells, "ding, dong! Why do you not come to church like others? Why are you not dressed in your Sunday clothes, and wherefore do you heave such doleful sighs, whilst we ring merrily? Ding, dong! ding, dong!"

"Is there not a cause?" replied the soldier. "This day I am turned out of home and heritage, though indeed I am the true heir."

"Nevertheless we shall ring for your return," said the bells.

As he went, the sun shone on the green fields, and in the soldier's eyes, and said, "See how brightly I shine! But you, comrade, why is your face so cloudy?"

"Is there not good reason?" replied he. "This day I am turned out of home and heritage, and yet I am the true heir."

"Nevertheless I shall shine on your return," said the sun.

Along the road the hawthorn hedges were white with blossom. "Heyday!" they cried, "who is this that comes trimp tramp, with a face as long as a poplar-tree? Cheer up, friend! It is spring!

sweet spring! All is now full of hope and joy, and why should you look so sour?"

"May I not be excused?" said the soldier. "This day I am turned out, of home and heritage, and yet I am the true heir."

"Nevertheless we shall blossom when you return," said the hedges.

When he had wandered for three days and three nights, all he had was spent, and there was no shelter to be seen but a dark gloomy forest, which stretched before him. Just then he saw a small, weazened old woman, who was trying to lift a bundle of sticks on to her back.

"That is too heavy for you, good mother," said the soldier; and he raised and adjusted it for her.

"Have you just come here?" muttered the old crone; "then the best thanks I can give you is to bid you get away as fast as you can."

"I never retreated yet, dame," said the soldier, and on he went.

Presently he met with a giant, who was strolling along by the edge of the wood, knocking the cones off the tops of the fir-trees with his finger-nails. He was an ill-favoured-looking monster, but he said, civilly enough, "You look in want of employment, comrade. Will you take service with me?"

"I must first know two things," answered the soldier; "my work and my wages."

"Your work," said the giant, "is to cut a path through this wood to the other side. But then you shall have a year and a day to do it in. If you do it within the time, you will find at the other end a magpie's nest, in which is the ring of which you are in search. The nest also contains the crown jewels which have been stolen, and if you take these to the king, you will need no further reward. But, on the other hand, if the work is not done within the time, you will thenceforth be my servant without wages."

"It is a hard bargain," said the soldier, "but need knows no law, and I agree to the conditions."

When he came into the giant's abode, he was greatly astonished to see the little weazened old woman. She showed no sign of recognizing him, however, and the soldier observed a like discretion. He soon discovered that she was the giant's wife, and much in dread of her husband, who treated her with great cruelty.

"To-morrow you shall begin to work," said the giant.

"If you please," said the soldier, and before he went to bed he carried in water and wood for the old woman.

"There's a kinship in trouble," said he.

Next morning the giant led him to a certain place on the outskirts of the forest, and giving him an axe, said, "The sooner you begin, the better, and you may see that it is not difficult." Saying which, he took hold of one of the trees by the middle, and snapped it off as one might pluck a flower.

"Thus to thee, but how to me?" said the soldier; and when the giant departed he set to work. But although he was so strong, and worked willingly, the trees seemed almost as hard as stone, and he made little progress. When he returned at night the giant asked him how he got on.

"The trees are very hard," said he.

"So they always say," replied the giant; "I have always had idle servants."

"I will not be called idle a second time," thought the soldier, and next day he went early and worked his utmost. But the result was very small. And when he came home, looking weary and disappointed, he could not fail to perceive that this gave great satisfaction to the giant.

Matters had gone on thus for some time, when one morning, as he went to work, he found the little old woman gathering sticks as before.

"Listen," said she. "He shall not treat you as he has treated others. Count seventy to the left from where you are working, and begin again. But do not let him know that you have made a fresh start. And do a little at the old place from time to time, as a blind." And before he could thank her, the old woman was gone. Without more ado, however, he counted seventy from the old place, and hit the seventieth tree such a blow with his axe, that it came crashing down then and there. And he found that, one after another, the trees yielded to his blows as if they were touch-wood. He did a good day's work, gave a few strokes in the old spot, and came home, taking care to look as gloomy as before.

Day by day he got deeper and deeper into the wood, the trees falling before him like dry elder twigs; and now the hardest part of his work was walking backwards and fowards to the giant's home, for the forest seemed almost interminable. But on the three hundred and sixty-sixth day from his first meeting with the giant, the soldier cut fairly through on to an open plain, and as the light streamed in, a magpie flew away, and on searching her nest, the soldier found his mother's wedding-ring. He also found many precious stones of priceless value, which were evidently the lost crown jewels. And as his term of service with the giant was now ended, he did not trouble himself to return, but with the ring and the jewels in his pocket set off to find his way to the capital.

He soon fell in with a good-humoured, fellow who showed him the way, and pointed out everything of interest on the road. As they drew near, one of the royal carriages was driving out of the city gates, in which sat three beautiful ladies who were the king's daughters.

"The two eldest are engaged to marry two neighbouring princes," said the companion.

"And whom is the youngest to marry?" asked the soldier, "for she is by far the most beautiful."

"She will never marry," answered his companion, "for she is pledged to the man who shall find the crown jewels, and cut a path through the stone-wood forest that borders the king's domains. And that is much as if she were promised to the man who should fetch down the moon for her to play with. For the jewels are lost beyond recall, and the wood is an enchanted forest."

"Nevertheless she shall be wed with my mother's ring," thought the soldier. But he kept his own counsel, and only waited till he had smartened himself up, before he sought an audience of the king.

His claim to the princess was fully proved; the king heaped honours and riches upon him; and he made himself so acceptable to his bride-elect, that the wedding was fixed for an early day.

"May I bring my old father, madam?" he asked of the princess.

"That you certainly may," said she. "A good son makes a good husband."

As he entered his native village the hedges were in blossom, the sun shone; and the bells rang for his return.

His stepmother now welcomed him, and was very anxious to go to court also. But her husband said, "No. You took such good care of the homestead, it is but fit you should look to it whilst I am away."

As to the giant, when he found that he had been outwitted, he went off, and was never more heard of in those parts. But the soldier took his wife into the city, and cared for her to the day of her death.

# THE MAGICIAN TURNED MISCHIEF-MAKER.

There was once a wicked magician who prospered, and did much evil for many years. But there came a day when Vengeance, disguised as a blind beggar, overtook him, and outwitted him, and stole his magic wand. With this he had been accustomed to turn those who offended him into any shape he pleased; and now that he had lost it he could only transform himself.

As Vengeance was returning to his place, he passed through a village, the inhabitants of which had formerly lived in great terror of the magician, and told them of the downfall of his power. But they only said, "Blind beggars have long tongues. One must not believe all one hears," and shrugged their shoulders, and left him.

Then Vengeance waved the wand and said, "As you have doubted me, distress each other;" and so departed.

By and by he came to another village, and told the news. But here the villagers were full of delight, and made a feast, and put the blind beggar in the place of honour; who, when he departed, said, "As you have done by me, deal with each other always!" and went on to the next village.

In this place he was received with even warmer welcome; and when the feast was over, the people brought him to the bridge which led out of the village, and gave him a guide-dog to help him on his way.

Then the blind beggar waved the wand once more and said;

"Those who are so good to strangers must needs be good to each other. But that nothing may be wanting to the peace of this place, I grant to the beasts and birds in it that they may understand the language of men."

Then he broke the wand in pieces, and threw it into the stream. And when the people turned their heads back again from watching the bits as they floated away, the blind beggar was gone.

Meanwhile the magician was wild with rage at the loss of his wand, for all his pleasure was to do harm and hurt. But when he came to himself he said: "One can do a good deal of harm with his tongue. I will turn mischief-maker; and when the place is too hot to hold me, I can escape in what form I please."

Then he came to the first village, where Vengeance had gone before, and here he lived for a year and a day in various disguises; and he made more misery with his tongue than he had ever accomplished in any other year with his magic wand. For every one distrusted his neighbour, and was ready to believe ill of him. So parents disowned their children, and husband and wives parted, and lovers broke faith; and servants and masters disagreed; and old friends became bitter enemies, till at last the place was intolerable even to the magician, and he changed himself into a cockchafer, and flew to the next village, where, Vengeance had gone before.

Here also he dwelt for a year and a day, and then he left it because he could do no harm. For those who loved each other trusted each other, and the magician made mischief in vain. In one of his disguises he was detected, and only escaped with his life from the enraged villagers by changing himself into a cockchafer and flying on to the next place, where Vengeance had gone before.

In this village he made less mischief than in the first, and more than in the second. And he exercised all his art, and changed his disguises constantly; but the dogs knew him under all.

One dog—the oldest dog in the place—was keeping watch over the miller's house, when he saw the magician approaching, in the disguise of an old woman.

"Do you see that old witch?" said he to the sparrows, who were picking up stray bits of grain in the yard. "With her evil tongue she is parting my master's daughter and the finest young fellow in the country-side. She puts lies and truth together, with more skill than you patch moss and feathers to build nests. And when she is asked where she heard this or that, she says, 'A little bird told me so.'"

"We never told her," said the sparrows indignantly, "and if we had your strength, Master Keeper, she should not malign us long!"

"I believe you are right!" said Master Keeper. "Of what avail is it that we have learned the language of men, if we do not help them to the utmost of our powers? She shall torment my young mistress no more."

Saying which he flew upon the disguised magician as he entered the gate, and would have torn him limb from limb, but that the mischief-maker changed himself as before into a cockchafer, and flew hastily from the village.

And thus he might doubtless have escaped to do yet further harm, had not three cock-sparrows overtaken him just before he crossed the bridge.

From three sides they hemmed him in, crying, "Which of us told you?" "Which of us told you?" "Which of us told you?"—and pecked him to pieces before he could transform himself again.

After which peace and prosperity befell all the neighbourhood.

## KNAVE AND FOOL.

A Fool and a Knave once set up house together; which shows what a fool the Fool was.

The Knave was delighted with the agreement; and the Fool thought himself most fortunate to have met with a companion who would supply his lack of mother-wit.

As neither of them liked work, the Knave proposed that they should live upon their joint savings as long as these should last; and, to avoid disputes, that they should use the Fool's share till it came to an end, and then begin upon the Knave's stocking.

So, for a short time, they lived in great comfort at the Fool's expense, and were very good company; for easy times make easy tempers.

Just when the store was exhausted, the Knave came running to the Fool with an empty bag and a wry face, crying, "Dear friend, what shall we do? This bag, which I had safely buried under a gooseberry-bush, has been taken up by some thief, and all my money stolen. My savings were twice as large as yours; but now that they are gone, and I can no longer perform my share of the bargain, I fear our partnership must be dissolved."

"Not so, dear friend," said the Fool, who was very good-natured; "we have shared good luck together, and now we will share poverty. But as nothing is left, I fear we must seek work."

"You speak very wisely," said the Knave, "And what, for instance, can you do?"

"Very little," said the Fool; "but that little I do well."

"So do I," said the Knave. "Now can you plough, or sow, or feed cattle, or plant crops?"

"Farming is not my business," said the Fool.

"Nor mine," said the Knave; "but no doubt you are a handicraftsman. Are you clever at carpentry, mason's work, tailoring, or shoemaking?"

"I do not doubt that I should have been had I learned the trades," said the Fool, "but I never was bound apprentice."

"It is the same with myself," said the Knave; "but you may have finer talents. Can you paint, or play the fiddle?"

"I never tried," said the Fool; "so I don't know."

"Just my case," said the Knave. "And now, since we can't find work, I propose that we travel till work finds us."

The two comrades accordingly set forth, and they went on and on, till they came to the foot of a hill, where a merchantman was standing by his wagon, which had broken down.

"You seem two strong men," said he, as they advanced; "if you will carry this chest of valuables up to the top of the hill, and down to the bottom on the other side, where there is an inn, I will give you two gold pieces for your trouble."

The Knave and the Fool consented to this, saying, "Work has found us at last;" and they lifted the box on to their shoulders.

"Turn, and turn about," said the Knave; "but the best turn between friends is a good turn; so I will lead the way up-hill, which is the hardest kind of travelling, and you shall go first down-hill, the easy half of our journey."

The Fool thought this proposal a very generous one, and, not knowing that the lower end of their burden was the heavy one, he carried it all the way. When they got to the inn, the merchant gave each of them a gold piece, and, as the accommodation was good, they remained where they were till their money was spent. After this, they lived there awhile on credit; and when that was exhausted, they rose one morning whilst the landlord was still in bed, and pursued their journey, leaving old scores behind them.

They had been a long time without work or food, when they came upon a man who sat by the roadside breaking stones, with a quart of porridge and a spoon in a tin pot beside him.

"You look hungry, friends," said he, "and I, for my part, want to get away. If you will break up this heap, you shall have the porridge for supper. But when you have eaten it, put the pot and spoon under the hedge, that I may find them when I return."

"If we eat first, we shall have strength for our work," said the Knave; "and as there is only one spoon, we must eat by turns. But fairly divide, friendly abide. As you went first the latter part of our journey, I will begin on this occasion. When I stop, you fall to, and eat as many spoonfuls as I ate. Then I will follow you in like fashion, and so on till the pot is empty."

"Nothing could be fairer," said the Fool; and the Knave began to eat, and went on till he had eaten a third of the porridge. The Fool, who had counted every spoonful, now took his turn, and ate precisely as much as his comrade. The Knave then began again, and was exact to a mouthful; but it emptied the pot. Thus the Knave had twice as much as the Fool, who could not see where he had been cheated.

They then set to work.

"As there is only one hammer," said the Knave, "we must work, as we supped, by turns; and as I began last time, you shall begin this. After you have worked awhile, I will take the hammer from you, and do as much myself whilst you rest. Then you shall take it up again, and so on till the heap is finished."

"It is not every one who is as just as you," said the Fool; and taking up the hammer, he set to work with a will.

The Knave took care to let him go on till he had broken a third of the stones, and then he did as good a share himself; after which the Fool began again, and finished the heap.

By this means the Fool did twice as much work as the Knave, and yet he could not complain.

As they moved on again, the Fool perceived that the Knave was taking the can and the spoon with him.

"I am sorry to see you do that, friend," said he.

"It's a very small theft," said the Knave. "The can cannot have cost more than sixpence when new."

"That was not what I meant," said the Fool, "so much as that I fear the owner will find it out."

"He will only think the things have been stolen by some vagrant," said the Knave—"which, indeed, they would be if we left them. But as you seem to have a tender conscience, I will keep them myself."

After a while they met with a farmer, who offered to give them supper and a night's lodging, if they would scare the birds from a field of corn for him till sunset.

"I will go into the outlying fields," said the Knave, "and as I see the birds coming, I will turn them back. You, dear friend, remain in the corn, and scare away the few that may escape me."

But whilst the Fool clapped and shouted till he was tired, the Knave went to the other side of the hedge, and lay down for a nap.

As they sat together at supper, the Fool said, "Dear friend, this is laborious work. I propose that we ask the farmer to let us tend sheep, instead. That is a very different affair. One lies on the hillside all day. The birds do not steal sheep; and all this shouting and clapping is saved."

The Knave very willingly agreed, and next morning the two friends drove a flock of sheep on to the downs. The sheep at once began to nibble, the dog sat with his tongue out, panting, and the Knave and Fool lay down on their backs, and covered their faces with their hats to shield them from the sun.

Thus they lay till evening, when, the sun being down, they uncovered their faces, and found that the sheep had all strayed away, and the dog after them.

"The only plan for us is to go separate ways in search of the flock," said the Knave; "only let us agree to meet here again." They accordingly started in opposite directions; but when the Fool was fairly off, the Knave returned to his place, and lay down as before.

By and by the dog brought the sheep back; so that, when the Fool returned, the Knave got the credit of having found them; for the dog scorned to explain his part in the matter.

As they sat together at supper, the Fool said, "The work is not so easy as I thought. Could we not find a better trade yet?"

"Can you beg?" said the Knave. "A beggar's trade is both easy and profitable. Nothing is required but walking and talking. Then one walks at his own pace, for there is no hurry, and no master, and the same tale does for every door. And, that all may be fair and equal, you shall beg at the front door, whilst I ask an alms at the back."

To this the Fool gladly agreed; and as he was as lean as a hunted cat, charitable people gave him a penny or two from time to time. Meanwhile, the Knave went round to the back yard, where he picked up a fowl, or turkey, or anything that he could lay his hands upon.

When he returned to the Fool, he would say, "See what has been given to me, whilst you have only got a few pence."

At last this made the Fool discontented, and he said, "I should like now to exchange with you. I will go to the back doors, and you to the front."

The Knave consented, and at the next house the Fool went to the back door; but the mistress of the farm only rated him, and sent him away. Meanwhile, the Knave, from the front, had watched her leave the parlour, and slipping in through the window, he took a ham and a couple of new loaves from the table, and so made off.

When the friends met, the Fool was crestfallen at his ill luck, and the Knave complained that all the burden of their support fell upon him. "See," said he, "what they give me, where you get only a mouthful of abuse!" And he dined heartily on what he had stolen; but the Fool only had bits of the breadcrust, and the parings of the ham.

At the next place the Fool went to the front door as before, and the Knave secured a fat goose and some plums in the back yard, which he popped under his cloak. The Fool came away with empty hands, and the Knave scolded him, saying, "Do you suppose that I mean to share this fat goose with a lazy beggar like you? Go on, and find for yourself." With which he sat down and began to eat the plums, whilst the Fool walked on alone.

After a while, however, the Knave saw a stir in the direction of the farm they had left, and he quickly perceived that the loss of the goose was known, and that the farmer and his men were in pursuit of the thief. So, hastily picking up the goose, he overtook the Fool, and pressed it into his arms, saying, "Dear friend, pardon a passing ill humour, of which I sincerely repent. Are we not partners in good luck and ill? I was wrong, dear friend; and, in token of my penitence, the goose shall be yours alone. And here are a few plums with which you may refresh yourself by the wayside. As for me, I will hasten on to the next farm, and see if I can beg a bottle of wine to wash down the dinner, and drink to our good-fellowship." And before the Fool could thank him, the Knave was off like the wind.

By and by the farmer and his men came up, and found the Fool eating the plums, with the goose on the grass beside him.

They hurried him off to the justice, where his own story met with no credit. The woman of the next farm came up also, and recognized him for the man who had begged at her door the day she lost a ham and two new loaves. In vain he said that these things also had been given to his friend. The friend never appeared; and the poor Fool was whipped and put in the stocks.

Towards evening the Knave hurried up to the village green, where his friend sat doing penance for the theft.

"My dear friend," said he, "what do I see? Is such cruelty possible? But I hear that the justice is not above a bribe, and we must at any cost obtain your release. I am going at once to pawn my own boots and cloak, and everything about me that I can spare, and if you have anything to add, this is no time to hesitate."

The poor Fool begged his friend to draw off his boots, and to take his hat and coat as well, and to make all speed on his charitable errand.

The Knave, took all that he could get, and, leaving his friend sitting in the stocks in his shirt-sleeves, he disappeared as swiftly as one could wish a man to carry a reprieve.

For those good folks to whom everything must be explained in full, it may be added that the Knave did not come back, and that he kept the clothes.

It was very hard on the Fool; but what can one expect if he keeps company with a Knave?

# UNDER THE SUN.

There once lived a farmer who was so avaricious and miserly, and so hard and close in all his dealings that, as folks say, he would skin a flint. A Jew and a Yorkshireman had each tried to bargain with him, and both had had the worst of it. It is needless to say that he never either gave or lent.

Now, by thus scraping, and saving, and grinding for many years, he had become almost wealthy; though, indeed, he was no better fed and dressed than if he had not a penny to bless himself with. But what vexed him sorely was that his next neighbour's farm prospered in all matters better than his own; and this, although the owner was as open-handed as our farmer was stingy.

When in spring he ploughed his own worn-out land, and reached the top of the furrow where his field joined one of the richly-fed fields of his neighbour, he would cast an envious glance over the hedge, and say, "So far and no farther?" for he would have liked to have had the whole under his plough. And so in the autumn, when he gathered his own scanty crop and had to stop his sickle short of the close ranks of his neighbour's corn, he would cry, "All this, and none of that?" and go home sorely discontented.

Now on the lands of the liberal farmer (whose name was Merryweather) there lived a dwarf or hillman, who made a wager that he would both beg and borrow of the covetous farmer, and out-bargain him to boot. So he went one day to his house, and asked him if he would kindly give him half a stone of flour to make hasty pudding with; adding, that if he would lend him a bag to carry it in to the hill, this should be returned clean and in good condition.

The farmer saw with half an eye that this was the dwarf from his neighbour's estate, and as he had always laid the luck of the liberal farmer to his being favoured by the good people, he resolved to treat the little man with all civility.

"Look you, wife," said he, "this is no time to be saving half a stone of flour when we may make our fortunes at one stroke. I have heard my grandfather tell of a man who lent a sack of oats to one of the fairies, and got it back filled with gold pieces. And as good measure as he gave of oats so he got of gold;" saying which, the farmer took a canvas bag to the flour-bin, and began to fill it. Meanwhile the dwarf sat in the larder window and cried—"We've a big party for supper to-night; give us good measure, neighbour, and you shall have anything under the sun that you like to ask for."

When the farmer heard this he was nearly out of his wits with delight, and his hands shook so that the flour spilled all about the larder floor.

"Thank you, dear sir," he said; "it's a bargain, and I agree to it. My wife hears us, and is witness. Wife! wife!" he cried, running into the kitchen, "I am to have anything under the sun that I choose to ask for. I think of asking for neighbour Merryweather's estate, but this is a chance never likely to happen again, and I should like to make a wise choice, and that is not easy at a moment's notice."

"You will have a week to think it over in," said the dwarf, who had come in behind him; "I must be off now, so give me my flour, and come to the hill behind your house seven days hence at midnight, and you shall have your share of the bargain."

So the farmer tied up the flour-sack, and helped the dwarf with it on to his back, and as he did so he began thinking how easily the bargain had been made, and casting about in his mind whether, he could not get more where he had so easily got much.

"And half a stone of flour is half a stone of flour," he muttered to himself, "and whatever it may do with thriftless people, it goes a long way in our house. And there's the bag—and a terrible lot spilled on the larder floor—and the string to tie it with, which doubtless he'll never think of returning—and my time, which must be counted, and nothing whatever for it all for a week to come." And the outlay so weighed upon his mind that he cleared his throat and began:

"Not for seven days, did you say, sir? You know, dear sir, or perhaps, indeed, you do not know, that when amongst each other we men have to wait for the settlement of an account, we expect something over and above the exact amount. Interest we call it, my dear sir."

"And you want me to give you something extra for waiting a week?" asked the dwarf. "Pray, what do you expect?"

"Oh, dear sir, I leave it to you," said the farmer. "Perhaps you may add some trifle—in the flour-bag, or not, as you think fit—but I leave it entirely to you."

"I will give you something over and above what you shall choose," said the dwarf; "but, as you say, I shall decide what it is to be." With which he shouldered the flour-sack, and went his way.

For the next seven days, the farmer had no peace for thinking, and planning, and scheming how to get the most out of his one wish. His wife made many suggestions to which he did not agree, but he was careful not to quarrel with her; "for," he said, "we will not be like the foolish couple who wasted three wishes on black-puddings. Neither will I desire useless grandeur and unreasonable elevation, like the fisherman's wife. I will have a solid and substantial benefit."

And so, after a week of sleepless nights and anxious days, he came back to his first thought, and resolved to ask for his neighbour's estate.

At last the night came. It was full moon, and the farmer looked anxiously about, fearing the dwarf might not be true to his appointment. But at midnight he appeared, with the flour-bag neatly folded in his hand.

"You hold to the agreement," said the farmer, "of course. My wife was witness. I am to have anything under the sun that I ask for; and I am to have it now."

"Ask away," said the dwarf.

"I want neighbour Merryweather's estate," said the farmer.

"What, all this land below here, that joins on to your own?"

"Every acre," said the farmer.

"Farmer Merryweather's fields are under the moon at present," said the dwarf, coolly, "and thus not within the terms of the agreement. You must choose again."

But as the farmer could choose nothing that was not then under the moon, he soon saw that he had been outwitted, and his rage knew no bounds at the trick the dwarf had played him.

"Give me my bag, at any rate," he screamed, "and the string—and your own extra gift that you promised. For half a loaf is better than no bread," he muttered, "and I may yet come in for a few gold pieces."

"There's your bag," cried the dwarf, clapping it over the miser's head like an extinguisher; "it's clean enough for a nightcap. And there's your string," he added, tying it tightly round the farmer's throat till he was almost throttled. "And, for my part, I'll give you what you deserve;" saying which he gave the farmer such a hearty kick that he kicked him straight down from the top of the hill to his own back door.

"If that does not satisfy you, I'll give you as much again," shouted the dwarf; and as the farmer made no reply, he went chuckling back to his hill.

Shian, a Gaelic name for fairy towers, which by day are not to be told from mountain crags.

Daoiné Shi (pronounced Dheener Shee) = Men of Peace.

Rung = a thick stick.

"In a compliment" = "as a present."

"Hoast" = cough.

"Brogues" = shoes.

"It's a far cry to Loch Awe."—Scotch Proverb.

Rath = a kind of moat-surrounded spot much favoured by Irish fairies. The ditch is generally overgrown with furze-bushes.

Printed in Great Britain
by Amazon

81261726R00047